Prince
of
DARKNESS

A JAZZ FICTION INSPIRED BY THE MUSIC OF MILES DAVIS

Dante to V[irgil]
"Does anyone descend to
Whose pain stems only from having
All hope cut off?"
Virgil to Dante:
"That place is the lowest and darkest,
And the farthest from the light.
But I have come back even from there."

(Adapted from Dante's *Inferno*, Canto 9)

20/20

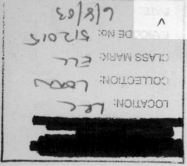

Pub..0
An imprint of The X Press
6 Hoxton Square, London, N1 6NU
Tel: 0171 729 1199
Fax: 0171 729 1771

Printed by Caledonian International Book Manufacturing Ltd, Glasgow, UK

Distributed in UK by Turnaround Distribution, Unit 3, Olympia Trading Estate, Coburg Road, London N22 6TZ
Tel: 0181 829 3000
Fax: 0181 881 5088

ISBN 1 874509 64 6

This book is dedicated with great appreciation
to
MARILYN LOWERY

Teacher, editor, mentor, agent, muse, and friend. And
everything she does, she does, as Pericles says of the Athenians,
with exceptional grace and versatility.

May 30, 1990

Merlin Black lurched toward the sunset. Dark like a storm cloud. Ominous like an off-shore hurricane. He felt, not so much warmed by the late spring heat, as awakened from a nightmare. He saw, not so much a blood-scarlet orb expunged by the curved and boundless horizon of the Pacific, as ambivalent proof that he was still alive.

Why had he agreed to give an interview? The bitch kept asking questions. The habit of indifference was hard to break. Better not to think. Better not to feel.

Merlin was dressed in white: white pants, white t-shirt, white gold chain around his neck. All white. Blinding white against the blackness of his skin.

His face, like a butte or a mesa, was carved from time and pain. His eyes burned holes in your soul, like lasers. Except they were hidden behind dark glasses, almost always. Perhaps those glasses turned the lasers inside. Maybe that's why he was so self-absorbed. The rays tore holes in his own soul like the vodka he drank, straight from the bottle, tore holes in his stomach.

Merlin fluttered, like a wounded butterfly, down to a resting place in the moist softness of the sand. The bottle of *Stoli* in his right hand now, always, as his trumpet used to be. He had agreed to play again. After five years of retirement. Why? He felt lost. He needed to talk. Call someone on the telephone. But who? His estranged wife? His ex-agent? His son, to whom he had not spoken in years?

A beautiful white woman in a bikini walked past. Then she stopped and turned back around.

"You're Merlin Black. Aren't you?"

"Yes."

"I'm a big fan. I have all your records."

"Thanks."

He watched her ass as she walked down the beach. Skimpy, snow-white material hardly concealed the soft bronze of her tanned skin. The sweet undulation of flesh in a rhythmic sway. The rhythm of jazz. The rhythm of life. When had all younger women become beautiful, he wondered. It hadn't been true when he was their age. And when had sexual attraction become more like pain than pleasure? When he was younger, he had assumed that by the time he reached sixty, he would no longer have a need for sex. He wished he didn't.

Merlin pulled off his t-shirt and wristwatch then ran to the edge and plunged into the surf. The cold startled him. The salt water stung. He was still alive.

Later, he called Peter Pollard, his long-time friend and arranger.

Peter was a thin wisp of a balding, white man, sixty, about Merlin's age, gentle and soft-spoken.

""I need your help for this Hollywood Bowl gig."

"You've got it, Merlin."

"I need some musicians."

"Well, Merlin, I can lend you some of mine. Are there any of your old band you want back?"

"No. I want to start over. I want to do something new."

"When do you want to start?"

"Soon. Can I call you back tomorrow?"

"Sure. And, Merlin?"

"Yeah?"

"I can't tell you how happy I am that you are coming out of retirement. You're the world's greatest jazz musician. And it has been a privilege to work with you."

"You're a bad motherfucker, Peter. But thanks for lying."

"I ain't lying, Merlin."

"Later, Peter."

"Later, man."

Merlin hung up and wandered into the bedroom. He disappeared into the closet and felt his way to the back corner. Finally, he discovered it. His trumpet case. He unsnapped the locks and pulled the horn out. He puckered his lips and spat drily, making certain he had the breath. Testing his chops. He fingered the keys. He put the trumpet to his mouth.

Kimberly Gates stopped her green VW Rabbit, behind his house, next to the garbage cans, in the narrow parking lot, just off the Pacific Coast Highway. She jerked her car keys out of the ignition and took a deep breath. Glancing in the rear-view mirror, she pulled her long, frizzy, red hair back into some semblance of order. The brightness of her alabaster skin, only slightly subdued by makeup. Not too shabby, she thought, for a forty year old broad. Considering.

She grabbed her purse and opened the door of her Rabbit to the swishing, swooshing noise of traffic. Every driver on the PCH felt obliged to treat the curving highway as if it were the Indianapolis 500. The second day of the Merlin Black interview couldn't be any worse than the first, she thought. Or could it? Yesterday, a mere half hour, seemed forever. Today would be much longer.

Not that Merlin didn't seem both compelling and even, in his own way, attractive. But difficult. Tense and occasionally hostile, he made her feel acutely uncomfortable. But she simply would not let him intimidate her. This interview could make her reputation. Give her the writing career she had always wanted.

But more than that, she knew Merlin was an important person. A man famous to all African-Americans as a symbol of uncompromising dignity. A man who refused to play Negro stereotypes, even in the days before the civil rights' movement, when it was expected. He never rolled his eyes or told jokes or acted dumb. Even now, he never pandered to the tastes or the expectations of a white audience. He was a strong, black prince, a stern and serious minded genius, who played music, not dance music, but searing, beautiful melodies.

The rear of Merlin Black's house, like most Malibu mansions, looked plain, a modest, unassuming shack. The luxury was all indoors and on the ocean-side front. Kimberly fought her way through the garbage cans, walked up the three steps to the back porch, and rang the doorbell. Nothing happened. After about three minutes, she rang it again, long and hard.

"What?" came the harsh reply, more an accusation than a question.

"It's Kimberly Gates."

Kimberly heard the sound of several dead-bolt locks being undone. The door creaked open as the wrinkled face of Merlin Black peered through the gap.

"Who?"

"Kimberly Gates? The interview for *Playboy*?"

Merlin didn't budge.

"We started yesterday," she said. "Kimberly Gates."

"Oh, yeah. Come in."

Kimberly pushed the door open and watched the retreating back of Merlin, naked to the waist, wearing only purple silk pyjama bottoms, as he walked out of the room. The walls of the large living room blazed with a dazzling white, like the sun drenched stucco of the buildings on Greek islands. The furniture, all black or dark brown, made a dramatic contrast.

Framed facsimiles of album covers and various awards decorated the walls. Several Grammies stood on the mantle above the fireplace, as well as an Academy Award he won for the background score to a movie, composed back in the late 60's.

Merlin walked back into the room, having slipped on a black sweatshirt with *New Orleans Jazz and Heritage Festival*, spelled out in red letters.

"Sit down," he said.

Kimberly chose a large brown leather chair next to a small table and lamp, situated in front of a large plate glass window with a spectacular view of the Pacific Ocean. She pulled a note pad and a small tape recorder out of her purse.

"Would you like a drink? Miss... What did you say your name was?" Merlin started to walk towards the bar.

"Gates. Kimberly."

"Gates Kimberly or Kimberly Gates?"

"Kimberly Gates. And I would love a Perrier."

"A what?" He turned around and looked at her as if he didn't know what she was talking about.

"Mineral water."

"I asked you if you wanted a drink."

"Look, Mr Black..."

"Merlin."

4

"Look, Merlin, I'm working. I'd love a glass of water. But if that's too much trouble, then, nothing. Thank you." Kimberly had no intention of telling Merlin that she did not drink. Could not drink. Had given it up, because she loved it too much.

"Don't you go gettin' angry and shit, now. I offered you a drink. I'm trying to be polite and hospitable. And you be all pissed off and shit." Merlin secretly grinned, as he slipped into jive talk. He loved to use it, especially with white chicks. It always made them get prim and stiff and begin to enunciate every word with great precision.

He went behind the bar. Merlin was proud of his roomy Malibu living room and the huge bar he had built in it.

"Everything in California seems to have so much more room," he said. "It's wonderful after all those years in cramped apartments in New York. Not only does this house have a great view of the Pacific Ocean, but it has space. I got so many rooms in this joint, I could almost get lost. And I got a bar in every one of them. But this one is a real motherfucker! Don't you think so?"

"Yes," Kimberly said timidly, not entirely certain if "motherfucker" was a good thing in this context.

"Look, it's seven feet of solid, chest-level mahogany, with wine racks, ice buckets, blenders, and everything that's even remotely connected with fixin' booze. And check out the refrigerator back here, it's got its own ice-maker."

"It's wonderful," Kimberly said.

He didn't mention the huge, rectangular mirror above the refrigerator. Merlin usually made a point of not looking in the mirror, but occasionally he forgot. He had aged badly. He had once been on the cover of *Life* and *Look* and had modeled the latest in men's fashion for *Esquire*. He had been considered handsome, hip, debonair — "the black Cary Grant."

Now his face was wrinkled like old leather. His hair was falling out. There were enormous bags under his eyes. Still vain about his appearance, Merlin simply refused to believe that *he* was the repulsive raisin he saw reflected behind the bar. He considered once taking the mirror out, but he loved the way it reflected the ocean and made his large house seem even more spacious.

Merlin fixed himself a vodka straight up, some of the

genuine Russian vodka, *Stoli*, plopped an olive in it, and pulled a cold bottle of Perrier out of the refrigerator for the white woman. He liked her looks, her pale skin, her long, red frizzy hair, and her pointed, Roman nose. So he decided to feel her out a little.

"I didn't know *Playboy* had any female reporters," he said.

"The CEO of *Playboy* is a woman."

He handed Kimberly the bottle of Perrier.

"You want a glass?"

"No, this is fine. Thank you."

"But I thought all you bitches were feminists now and didn't put up with none of that chauvinist *Playboy* shit."

"Look, Mr... I mean, Merlin. Do you like it when I say all black people are like this or like that?"

"It don't matter whether I like it or not. You gonna say it anyway. Ain't you?" Merlin drank the vodka quickly, walked back to the bar, and poured himself another.

"That's not fair."

"Oh," he said. "I'm sorry, Kimberly. May I call you Kimberly?"

"Please." Her soft voice could not disguise the fact that she was making a supreme effort to control her anger.

"It's not exactly fair either, Kimberly, when they beat up my brothers in Mississippi or kill them in South Africa. But let me rephrase the question. How come you working for a racist, sexist outfit like *Playboy* magazine?"

"I'm a writer. It's a gig. That's all. Can you understand that? Besides I'm supposed to be asking you questions."

"Okay, Kimberly. Can I ask you one more question before we get back to work?"

"Yes."

"Will you have dinner with me tonight?"

As he asked the question, Kimberly realized something remarkable was happening. He was smiling. She'd never seen him smile before. Everything she'd read about him emphasized that he never smiled in public or mugged or did that Louis Armstrong 'grin-for-the-honkies' routine.

But he smiled for her. It transformed his whole face. It made him look decades younger. It seemed to say: 'All that other stuff is just an act. I'm not angry. I'm just playing a game with you. A little joke. Don't you get it'?

6

"Yes," Kimberly said, in answer to Merlin's dinner invitation.

He'd expected more resistance from her. She accepted too quickly. She must have something up her sleeve, he thought.

"Great," he said. "Now, what you wanna know?"

"Why are you so cynical, Merlin?"

"Cynical? Me? What makes you think I'm cynical?"

Kimberly turned the pages of her note pad.

"Well, yesterday you said… Let me see, where is it? Oh, yeah. Here, it is. Yesterday, you said, and I quote: 'If the whole human race was tied up to one of those hospital life support systems, and I had the power, I'd unplug the motherfucker and put everybody out of their misery'."

"You call that cynical, Kimberly? I'd just call it the proper medicine for an incurable disease. Now, ask me something more important."

"Okay. Why did you decide to come out of retirement?"

Merlin thought about the question, as he sipped the second vodka and looked out at the waves pounding the shore. He used to believe California was a jive-ass sort of place. Lots of surfers, bleach blondes, and airhead Nazis. If it didn't fucking happen in New York, he thought, then it just wasn't happening. Period!

But after I put my horn down five years ago, he thought, I just… I don't know. I just lost interest in what was happening, I guess. The people here are not as uptight. Not as hostile. But it's not even that so much. Not the people. It's here. This place. On the beach. Sitting on the beach and looking at the ocean the way folks been doing for thousands of years. The way the Indians used to do before the jive-ass white man covered everything in concrete and polluted the whole basin. But in spite of their efforts, it was still possible to love the beauty of the water. When I first moved out here, I used to get hypnotized by the waves. Course, I was using a lot of shit back then. I was fucked up, most of the time.

"I was fucked up most of the time," he said out loud, because he realized it had been quite a while since he'd said anything to Miss Gates, Kimberly.

"When, Merlin? When were you fucked up most of the time?" She put down her note pad and turned on the tape recorder. Merlin didn't much like the idea of having his conversation taped, but he had agreed to it up front, and he didn't like to go back on his word.

"When I quit playing, back in '85. That's when I was fucked up most of the time. But it wasn't smack, like them white newspapers said it was. I quit that shit a long time ago. Right after Charlie Parker died. That cured me of smack. I never put another needle in my arm after Bird died. That cured me for good. I just mainly did coke, uppers and downers, and shit like that. And booze, of course. Lots of booze."

"Was that why you retired? Because you were strung out?"

"No, chick. That's not why I quit: ' 'Cause I was strung out'."

"I'd appreciate it if you didn't call me a 'chick'."

"Yes ma'am," he said. And then there was that smile again. Kimberly didn't want to let her guard down, but the smile was definitely disarming. It was as if she had called his bluff, and he had acknowledged her superior gamesmanship. He walked over to the stereo and looked into the cabinet where he stored all his CDs.

"I quit because I didn't have anything new to say. I'd been playing trumpet since I was ten years old. That was forty-five years. It just wasn't coming. It felt old. It felt corny. It felt like I'd said it all. Played it all before."

He showed her a copy of a CD entitled *Afro-Jamaican Jazz*. It had a picture of Merlin with computer-generated dreadlocks playing a trumpet by an idyllic beach next to an aquamarine ocean.

"Ever heard this one?"

"Sure," she said.

"This was just one of five albums I recorded in 1985 alone."

"I know. The critics say that was one of your peak periods. That you were changing styles so fast that nobody could keep up."

"The critics don't know jack-shit. If you're going to understand music... If you're going to understand me, you gotta get that one thing straight, honey. Critics couldn't find their way out of their own assholes with a flashlight. I was changing styles because I was bored. Bored with all the shit."

"Like what?"

"Like the critics for one thing. Now, they say it was some of my best music. But that's not what they were saying then. *Then*, they were saying I was crazy, and that the music was noise, and that I had lost it."

"So, you quit because it wasn't fun anymore?" Kimberly's eyes strayed toward the east wall of the living room. She again studied some of Merlin's awards and the framed album covers, preferring to avoid his intense scrutiny.

"Yeah, that and because Cheryl died."

He pulled another CD from the shelf. He showed her the case with its title, *Love For Sale*, in large letters. It preserved the original cover, a photograph of Cheryl taken thirty years earlier. Her light, smooth, cafe-au-lait skin and huge, brown eyes revealed a beauty that had not diminished over the years. Had not dimmed with changing fashions.

"Pretty wasn't she?"

"Beautiful. This is Cheryl?"

"Yep," he said, putting the CD back on the shelf.

"Your second wife?"

"Well, it depends on how you're counting them, honey. See, I never was really married to Harriet."

"Please don't call me 'honey'." Kimberly, although touched by Merlin's obvious affection for his dead wife, was equally determined to defend herself from any insult or outrageous comment he lobbed her way.

"Shit!" Merlin said in mock exasperation.

"Harriet is the mother of your two children?"

"Yeah, that's right, Gates, Kimberly. The mother of my two children. Although only one of 'em's still alive."

"Please don't call me Gates, Kimberly."

"You kinda testy, ain't ya? Kinda hard to get along with? Is that what they say about me — that I'm hard to get along with?"

"Actually, my editor didn't use the word 'hard'. I believe her word was 'impossible'."

"Your editor is a bitch too?"

"You know, Merlin, studies show that approximately one hundred per cent of the women interviewed find that word offensive."

"Well, lessee. I can't call you a bitch. Can't call you 'honey'. Can't call you a chick. Can't even call you Gates, Kimberly. What the fuck am I supposed to call you?"

"What about just Kimberly, Mr... that is, Merlin."

"Well, okay, 'Just Kimberly'. But while we're being fussy about names... Although I admit you're making progress. You stopped calling me Mr Black. And I'm sure that was hard for you, since I am black. And so to call me 'black' reinforces your sense of racial superiority. I've found that to be especially true with redheads. But I asked you to call me by my first name. So now you've made it to Mr Merlin. Maybe you'd rather call me 'Uncle Tom'?"

"Tell me about Harriet, Merlin."

"I can't wait to read this jive-ass interview in your white, pussy-magazine. I bet it starts off: 'The craggy, grumpy, old, black buck was difficult to get along with'. Naw, not 'difficult' — 'The motherfucker was impossible!' Do you mind if I have another drink?"

"No."

" 'Scuse me." Merlin got up and stalked back to the bar.

"You are very generous for a white person."

"Tell me about Harriet, Merlin." Kimberly found it difficult to keep a straight face. Merlin seemed less like King Kong now and more like the Cowardly Lion from *The Wizard of Oz*.

Merlin poured another *Stoli*, paused a second, and then made it a double.

"How come you so cool? How come you don't tell me to piss off and storm outta here like all the others done?"

"You'd like that, wouldn't you, Merlin?"

Merlin drank his vodka and stared at Gates, Kimberly. She's not young, he thought, but pretty. And spirited. He sensed passion just beneath the surface. He felt that, even though she'd dressed in a long, green skirt and big, horn-rimmed glasses. The only thing about her he didn't like were her thin lips. Merlin liked full, sensuous lips. Kimberly's seemed thin, even for a Caucasian.

Unlike a lot of the black cats he'd played with, including Charlie 'Bird' Parker, Merlin had never much cared for white women. He was much more attracted to black women. The women in his life, the ones he really loved — Harriet, the mother of his children, Cheryl, the dancer, and Tara, the actress — were all African-American.

White chicks seemed easier to get along with, though, he thought. Black bitches had nasty tempers. At least, all the ones he'd ever met. Beginning with his mother. She was the worst.

Worse even than Tara.

Merlin walked back to the stereo complex.

"Any of my CDs you don't have?"

"Yeah, *Live From the Village Vanguard*. I haven't been able to find that one anywhere."

"Volume one or two?"

"Either."

"Here." He handed her both CDs.

"Thank you, Merlin." She was both surprised and gratified. Merlin kept jumping back from rude to gracious, keeping her constantly off-guard.

"They're Japanese imports. Hard to find."

"Will you autograph them for me?"

"Sure."

Merlin found a pen.

"I'm never sure where to sign a CD."

"On the inside flap will be fine."

He took the CDs over to the bar, snapped open the lids, and autographed the papers inside.

"Where you from Just Kimberly?"

"Right here in Los Angeles."

"How come you so white then. I thought maybe you were from Mississippi." She did have the palest skin he'd ever seen.

"I can't help it, Merlin. I was born this way." Kimberly started rummaging around in her black, leather handbag. "Is race the only thing you like to talk about?"

"No, Just Kimberly, I also like to talk about sex and music. Which one of those topics appeals to you?"

"When Cheryl died, weren't you still married to Tara?" Kimberly found what she was looking for, a plastic bottle of Extra Strength Bufferin. She quickly swallowed two of the white capsules and washed them down with her Perrier.

"Am I giving you a headache, Kim?"

"No," she said automatically. Then she looked up at him and smiled. "What would you have said, if I'd said 'yes'?"

"I'd ask you if you were still going to have dinner with me? I plan to make reservations at Spago's." He handed her the autographed CDs. "Are you?"

"Yes, of course. I wouldn't dream of turning down an invitation to Spago's. Besides, I have a proposition to make." She put the CDs and the Bufferin back into her handbag. "Not a sexual one," she said quickly, as an afterthought.

"Well, fuck me twice on Sunday!" Merlin said. He took another sip of his vodka. He went back behind the bar again. It made him feel safe. Like he was inside a fortress, and could afford to fire off his cannons, without fear of retribution. "I was hoping you wanted to give me a blow job."

"No, Merlin. That isn't it."

"Lots of bitches do, you know. I have to beat them off with a stick sometimes. They just dying to suck my black cock!"

"I'm sure." Kimberly looked down at his brown wall-to-wall carpeting. It made quite a contrast to the walls. Merlin always said he liked to keep his whites up against the wall.

"Maybe you'd, at least, like to see my dick, first, before you make up your mind for sure? You might just fall in love with the motherfucker. Want me to whip it out?"

"No. No," Kimberly said. "I'm quite certain on that point. No pun intended."

"Damn!" Merlin said, before downing the rest of his *Stoli*.

"It's enough to drive a man to booze! Besides, mine ain't no point, honey. It's more like a fuckin' peninsula."

"Tell me more about Harriet."

"Well, I knocked Harriet up twice, the first time was even before I left Memphis. I used to be over at her house all the time. It was hard in those days. The Ku Klux Klan everywhere. White kids would beat you up, just 'cause you was black."

The two white guys were both bigger than he was. Merlin didn't want trouble. Not tonight. He had been looking forward to this night for weeks. His parents were going to Arkansas to visit his grandmother. Merlin could have the house to himself. That is, he and Harriet could have the house to themselves. They could make love in a bed for the first time.

The two shapes came closer. They were wearing stocking caps, ear muffs, and heavy coats, but he could tell that they were white. It was a chilly winter night. It had, in fact, snowed earlier in the day, but it hadn't settled.

Merlin pulled the bill of his red and green plaid cap down in front of his face, stuck his hands in his pocket, and looked down toward the sidewalk. His short, slight build was easy prey for bullies. He was fourteen years old but barely looked twelve. Edgar Black, his father, had blamed him for being badly beaten up by three white kids the previous summer. His father told him that, if he got in trouble with white kids again, not even to bother to come home. Merlin had tried to explain that it wasn't his fault, but his father wouldn't listen.

The two shapes came closer.

"Hey, nigger," the taller of the two white boys said.

"Yes?" Merlin did not look them in the face, and he stayed as far away as he could, without actually standing in the street.

"Yes, what?" the other boy asked.

"I don't know," Merlin said, inching his way down the grass next to the sidewalk.

"You say 'Yes, sir', when you talkin' to a white man."

"Yes, sir," Merlin said, still shuffling away.

"And stand still, when we're talkin' to you."

Merlin stood still and stared down at his new, black-lace, Sunday shoes. He wore an overcoat on top of his best suit and tie. He and Harriet had told her mother, Mrs Loomis, that they were going to the high school Christmas dance. That's why Merlin was so dressed-up. If his Sunday suit got ruined, his father would kill him.

"What you doin' in this neighborhood, boy?"

"I live here."

"You live here... *WHAT*?"

"Sir," Merlin said, looking up at his tormentors for the first time. A tuft of hair peeked out of the stocking cap of the taller one. The other boy had bad acne and a twisted nose.

"You live here — on Washington?"

His father, Edgar Black, was proud that their new, red-brick house was on Washington. Far from Beale Street, far from the honky tonks, far from the squalid black neighborhoods. It was modest by white standards, but luxurious compared to the shotgun shacks where most of Memphis' black population lived. Usually, Merlin too was proud of his home.

"Yes sir, I live on Washington," he said.

"I didn't know niggers lived on our street. Did you, Pete?"

"Naw, Buster. The only nigger I know of on Washington is that trouble-making lawyer nigger. You ain't that nigger's pickaninny, are you?"

Merlin stuck his hands deeper in his coat pocket and stared down at his shoes again.

"Hey, nigger," Pete said. "Buster just asked you a question. Are you related to that nigger lawyer on Washington?"

"I'm sorry. I have to go, sir." Merlin set off running. Harriet's house was only three blocks away, up on Poplar. Merlin heard the boys behind him, even before Buster yelled:

"You better stop, nigger, or we gonna beat shit outta you."

Merlin did not look back. His arms and his legs were pumping fast. His breath hurt as he took the rapid, cold air in, deep down to his lungs. Please God, he thought, don't let them catch me this time.

He turned onto Poplar and saw cars moving in both directions. But that was not much assurance. A white man would not stop another white man from beating up a colored person. Merlin could still hear the running footsteps behind him. There was a stoplight on the next corner. Merlin ran toward the light just as it was turning red. He ran right out into the street and threw himself directly in front of a blue 1939 Oldsmobile that was just coming to a stop.

"Whoa!" the driver cried. "What you doin', stupid nigger?"

Merlin walked back toward the sidewalk and saw that Pete and Buster had stopped. They hadn't gone away, but they were no longer moving.

"I be real sorry, sir," Merlin said to the driver in a slow, exaggerated Uncle Tom accent.

14

"These damn niggers," the driver said, apparently to his windshield. "Ain't got the sense God gave to a mule!" He looked over at Merlin. "Now, looka here, pickaninny. Stay out of the street. If I hit you and kill you, they'll take away my licence. Even if you ain't no smarter than a monkey. You hear?"

"Yes sir, I be's mo' careful in de few-chah." Merlin was mocking him, but the driver, a nearly bald man in his fifties, didn't catch the sarcasm. The light changed and he drove off. Pete and Buster had disappeared.

Harriet lived with her mother in a wooden, whitewashed shack. The one-storey building was set off the ground by thin, red-brick blocks, but the entire structure was as unstable as it was unsightly. Whereas Merlin's front porch was roofed, solid, and supported by stone, Harriet's was rickety and open, its thin roof held up by two small columns.

Merlin was vaguely aware that he was better off than Harriet, but he didn't give it much thought. Harriet's house was so typical of the type of place where most of Memphis' black population lived, that it did not seem odd to him.

"Oh hi, Merlin," Harriet said when she opened the door.

"Harriet, can I come in quick?"

"Sure. But I thought we were going to the dance." Harriet's short, kinky hair and oval-shaped head sat uncomfortably on her long, thin body. She was wearing her best party dress, a demure, soft pink, with a virginal, white lace collar.

"Harriet, let me in. Right now!"

"Okay. Okay." She sensed the note of panic in his voice.

Merlin walked in the living room and looked around.

"Where's your mama?"

"She's doing the dishes." But at that moment, Mrs Loomis walked into the room, drying her hands on her apron.

"I hear you two are going to the Christmas dance." Mrs Loomis looked like an older version of her daughter, except her body had filled out enough to fit her oval-shaped head.

"Yes ma'am."

"Would you like a cup of hot chocolate before you go?"

"Yes ma'am."

Merlin stalled over his hot chocolate for about twenty minutes. He knew Buster and Pete wouldn't wait for him outside in the cold any longer than that.

Suddenly, he jumped up from the sofa, where he had been

15

sitting.

"We better be on our way now. We're running a little late."

Harriet fetched her overcoat and held it out for Merlin to help her with. Merlin forced the sleeves down her arms with a frenzied jerk.

"Not so rough, Merlin," Harriet said irritably, "that's my new coat. Not some old gunnysack."

"Well, okay," Mrs Loomis said. "You two have a good time. Don't forget your mittens, now. It's plenty cold tonight."

"What's wrong with you, Merlin?" Harriet asked, as soon as they were outside. "First, you 'bout knock me down, getting inside the house. And then you act like you got ants in your pants and can't wait to leave."

Merlin stopped as soon as they were out of sight of the Loomis house and pulled Harriet into his arms. He kissed her long and passionately on the lips.

"It's because I want you so bad, Harriet," he said. "I can't wait to be alone with you." He did not want to tell her about Pete and Buster for fear she would be afraid to come with him. And Merlin did want to fuck her. It had become almost an obsession. They had been making love on the sly for several months now, and Merlin was hooked.

"Well, be nice then. You s'posed to be gentle with an expectant mother."

Merlin was thunderstruck. He looked her straight in the eyes.

"You sure?" he asked.

"Sure."

"Oh, shit!"

Merlin grabbed her arm and propelled her down the sidewalk toward Washington. Merlin knew that the possibility existed that Harriet could get pregnant. But his mind was not prepared to deal with the fact. He wanted to sleep with her but he did not want to marry her. He did not want to be tied down with a family in Memphis. He wanted to be playing his trumpet in New York.

"I ask you to be gentle with me, Merlin. And you drag me around like a sack of cotton."

Neither of them spoke again until they got to Merlin's house. Merlin hung up both of their coats in the closet in the small hallway between the front door and the living room. He

16

sat down on the long sofa which occupied most of the south side of the big room, the side next to the front window.

The Black house had fine, big panes of glass in its largest window, unlike the small window in the Loomis house, stuffed with paper and cardboard.

"Well?" Harriet said, standing impatiently in the middle of the room, in front of the piano.

"I tell you I'm gonna have your baby. You say an ugly word and then don't say nothing else. You s'posed to be happy. You s'posed to say something nice to me."

"Who says 'I s'posed'?" Merlin said, throwing his tie on the brown coffee table.

"I say. That's who. Merlin don't you love me? You said you did."

"Sure, I love you." Merlin looked up into Harriet's angry face. "Well, I do. I love you. But I ain't ready to settle down. I got plans."

"What plans?"

"My horn. You know, Harriet. My music."

Harriet sat down next to Merlin on the sofa.

"Music is a hobby, Merlin. You can't have a family and make a living off music."

"That reminds me," Merlin said, popping up off the sofa.

"What time is it now?"

"How would I know what time it is? It ain't like I got some fancy wristwatch or something."

"It must be past 7:30. It's time for 'The Sounds of Harlem', on the radio."

"Merlin, I think we have some things to talk about."

"Hush, now." Merlin was on his knees before the large brown wood, floor model radio in the dining room. The Black dining room was adjacent to the living room and was separated only by large, sliding doors which usually, as now, stood open. Merlin fiddled with the knobs until he found the right station.

The sweet music of Duke Ellington's 'In A Mellotone' came through the speaker. The creamy saxes sang out over the plucking bass, and the repeated one-note arpeggios, hammered out on the piano. Merlin was in heaven.

"Shit-fire," he said, "it's the Duke!"

"Don't talk that way in front of me," Harriet said, as she lay back down on the sofa in exasperation.

The music on the radio changed. A new song began with the ominous undertone of the baritone sax. Then three trombones with plunger mutes growled out a loud and slightly obscene, answering theme.

"That's 'Ko-Ko'," Merlin said. "It's a goddamn masterpiece. One of Duke's best numbers. But, shit, I wish Cootie Williams was still with the band."

"Who's Cootie Williams?" Harriet asked, kicking off her party shoes and plopping her feet up on the armrest of the sofa.

" 'Who's Cootie Williams'?" Merlin echoed in astonished disbelief. "Shit, girl! Cootie's just the best damn trumpet player who ever lived. Better than Armstrong. And a damn sight better than Harry James. Haven't you ever heard 'Concerto for Cootie'?"

"No."

"He was with Ellington, until that fuckin' honky Benny Goodman stole him away."

"Merlin Black, if you don't stop using that vile, low-down, filthy, gutter language, I'm going to go home. Do you hear me?"

"Yeah, yeah, Harriet. I hear." But what Merlin really heard was a thumping bass, a clarinet obbligato, mellow saxes, barking trombones, and above the din of all the rest — trumpets.

Trumpets! Trumpets blaring out gorgeous, boisterous trills that made Merlin's spine tingle and his heart race. Better than anything Gabriel or any other honky angel could even imagine. And it was not coming from heaven, but from some place infinitely better. It was coming from some mysterious place called the Savoy Ballroom in Harlem, on the island of Manhattan, in the fabulous Big Apple of New York City.

Harlem was a place in Merlin's mind more real than any White Christian Heaven. It was a place full of black people, where there were no Petes or Busters. And no parents with their humiliating put-downs and their unreasonable demands. And no pregnant Harriets, bitching and complaining and trying to get him to give up his horn. No, in Harlem all the cats were cool and all the chicks were solid.

Merlin was hypnotized by this programme, coming live from the center of the music world, from the center of everything that was hip and beautiful and swinging and marvelous. Where Merlin wanted to go. Where Merlin had to go if he was serious about his trumpet. And he was. He wanted to be a musician more than anything. More than fucking Harriet. More than getting revenge on white boys like Pete and Buster who were always picking on him. More than proving to his father that he amounted to something. More than getting away from his boozy mother... Well, more than anything.

"That's Ray Nance and Rex Stewart on trumpets," Merlin said.

"And I think Wallace Jones. They're good. But not as good as Cootie."

"This is Ron Taft," said the voice on the radio. "Coming to you live from the Savoy Ballroom. Speaking for Ivy Anderson, our featured soloist, and all the boys in Duke Ellington's Famous Orchestra, we'd like to bid you a fond farewell by playing a smash-hit number and Duke's brand new theme song. The song that tells you how to get to Harlem. If you wanna come to the Savoy Ballroom up in Harlem... Then you will surely... You *must* surely — 'Take The A-Train'."

The unison saxes blared out the familiar theme over Duke's rhythmic piano, as the announcer returned to the mike. "But don't touch that dial. More great music is coming your way, as we switch live to the Cafe Royal in the Hotel Pennsylvania, where Chesterfield Cigarettes is proud to present to you — Artie Shaw and his orchestra."

Merlin went back to the living room and flung himself on top of Harriet's reclining body. "Baby," he said. "I can't stop thinking about you."

"Seems to me, you been thinking more about Cootie Williams than you been thinking about me."

Merlin began to kiss her lightly on the neck and cheek.

"I want to make love to you, Harriet."

"I think we ought to talk about the baby, Merlin."

"We can do that anytime, Harriet. But how often do we get the house to ourselves? I want to make love to you in a bed and before my parents come home."

"All right, Merlin. But you got to get up. If I get this dress all wrinkled, mama will kill me."

Merlin stood up and helped Harriet off with her dress. He

then proceeded to take off the rest of her clothes. He hung the pink party dress up in the hall closet, but left everything else on the sofa.

Merlin gathered Harriet in his arms and carried her upstairs to his bedroom. As his passion mounted, he tore off his own clothes with wreckless speed. He lay down beside her and began kissing her again, this time with greater intensity and passion. He had only just entered her when he heard the front door burst open.

There was the sound of footsteps and then he heard his mother's voice.

"Merlin! Merlin Black! If you're upstairs, you'd better come down right this minute!"

"Oh, shit!" Merlin said.

"What am I s'posed to do?" Harriet whispered.

"I'll go down," Merlin said, jumping out of bed and throwing on his clothes, "you get dressed."

"How am I s'posed to do that?" Harriet hissed. "All my clothes are down stairs."

"Oh, yeah," Merlin said, "don't worry. I'll get them for you."

"And whose undergarments are these, Merlin?" Sarah Black asked her son, as soon as he walked down the stairs and into the living room.

Merlin looked at Harriet's white slip, her abandoned nylons, and her underwear, spread out all over the sofa. Speechless, he looked back into his mother's face which was soft, even now, when she was angry. It had a sad, repressed look to it. At thirty-five, Sarah Black still had her youthful looks, although her figure had filled out considerably from her childhood days.

She had a large forehead that showed no wrinkles. Her eyes and eyebrows were far apart across a broad nose. She had a large mouth and full, sensuous lips. Her hair was straightened and piled up artificially on the top of her head.

"Answer me, boy!" She seemed more than angry. She was outraged, and hurt as well.

"They belong to Harriet Loomis."

"What is that hussy doing in my house?"

"We thought you'd be gone longer," Merlin said weakly, trying to gather up Harriet's clothes.

"Obviously," Edgar Black said. Merlin's father was dressed in a conservative, but double-breasted, business suit. He was thin and erect, and his face had stern features. There was a thin whisper of a moustache under his long, pointed nose. He had an air of military precision, highlighted by his square jaw and very short hair. The only soft features of his face were the long, almost feminine, eyelashes.

"This time you've really done it. I'm taking the strap to you."

With one quick movement, Edgar pulled his belt off his waist and cracked it in the air.

"Wait a minute, Edgar. I want that strumpet out of my house first." Sarah took off her long, formal black coat and hung it up in the hall closet.

"You mean me, Mrs Black?" Harriet had found Merlin's bathrobe. She came down the stairs and into the living room, as if she were the Queen of Sheba.

"Get out of my house, young lady," Sarah said.

"Perhaps you wouldn't take that tone," Harriet said, jerking her clothes out of Merlin's arms. "If you knew I was going to give birth to your first grandchild."

As Harriet bounced back upstairs to get dressed, Sarah stared at her son in open-mouthed disbelief.

"Merlin, is this really true?"

"I don't know, mama. I guess so, if she says it is."

Sarah stood for a second, staring at her son, hurt and incredulous. Tears formed in the corners of her eyes. Her mood changed instantaneously, and then, without warning, she stormed out of the room in a blind fury.

"I want you to take Harriet home immediately," Edgar Black said. "Then you get yourself right back here and we'll have this out tonight, before anyone goes to bed."

"Why did you have to tell them?" Merlin asked Harriet later, as he was walking her home.

"I heard your mama calling me a hussy. I didn't think that was a nice way to start a relationship with my future mother-in-law. Besides, I've heard some stuff about her too."

"What have you heard about my mama?"

"Stuff. All about how she gets drunk a lot and acts crazy in public places. But don't you worry. I'll be nice to her. Long as she don't call me no more names. I'll be a perfect little daughter-in-law." Harriet squeezed Merlin's arm, looking him straight in the face and beamed him a broad smile.

"Harriet, I have plans."

"Well, I hope you do, Merlin Black," Harriet said as they finally reached the front door of the Loomis house. "I'm pregnant. You have to marry me. We settle down. You make all the plans you want to about getting a job and going to work. That's the way it's got to be, ain't it?"

"I don't know. My father's gonna beat the stuffing out of me."

Harriet kissed Merlin good night, lightly on the cheek and then on the lips. She smelled good. Like hazelnut.

By now the night was freezing cold. As much as Merlin was afraid to go home, he had no desire to stay outside. His mind was numb. He could not accept Harriet's pregnancy, nor the future she envisioned for them both.

He did not know how to deal with his angry parents. He did not know what he could say to them to explain his past behavior or his future ambitions. His father had always been disappointed with him. Merlin could never do anything to live up to his father's high expectations.

His mother was another, and even worse problem. He could not deal with her drinking or her sorrow. He wanted to get away from her. She scared him most of all.

Merlin had forgotten all about Pete and Buster when he turned the corner at Washington, and they appeared, as out of nowhere, in front of him.

"Lookey here, Buster," Pete said. "It's that uppity nigger."

"Are you sure, Pete? Might be one of those damn Japs what bombed Pearl Harbor."

"It ain't no Jap. It's that goddamn nigger lawyer's son. The one what was so disrespectful to us earlier this evening."

"I guess you're right, Pete. The light's not so good tonight."

Merlin's adrenalin shot sky-high. He tried to turn around and run, but Pete caught his right arm. He pinned both of Merlin's arms behind his back, and Buster was in his face.

"You're gonna have to learn some manners, nigger. If you want to live next to the good white people of Memphis."

"Let me go," Merlin cried. "I haven't done anything to you."

"Oh, yes you have, nigger. You have offended us deeply."

Merlin saw Buster's fist come toward him. He squirmed to free himself from Pete's firm hold, but he could not get away. The first blow was to the stomach, the second broke his nose.

Kimberly was excited about going to Spago's, the ritzy 'nouvelle cuisine' restaurant that propelled super-chef Wolfgang Puck to international fame. She had always wanted to eat there. She had seen it featured in magazines and on T.V. shows, like 'Lifestyles of the Rich and Famous'. She expected it to be crowded with famous people: Hollywood stars, writers, models, athletes, and politicians.

Merlin plopped the keys of his Jaguar into the valet's hands and escorted her inside. The receptionist showed the couple to a table by the window with a view of the lights and billboards of Sunset Boulevard, and, indeed, the entire city beyond that. The waiter took their drink orders and left them large, red menus.

"Okay. Kimberly, I've waited long enough. Tell me. What is this proposition you mentioned earlier? I'm dying of curiosity."

The waiter returned with the drinks, and Kimberly took a sip of her mineral water. She placed the glass back on the table and turned it around and around by the base of the stem.

"Have you ever thought about writing your autobiography?"

"Autobiography?" Merlin loosened his tie and shifted his weight around on the seat.

"Yeah, the story of your life."

"I know what the word means. Not all of us niggers are illiterate, you know?"

"I will not dignify that comment with a reply." Kimberly noticed that Merlin was dressed to the nines. He had on a black suit, a black bow tie, and a white, frilly shirt. She was still wearing the same green skirt and yellow blouse, but to Merlin she looked even prettier in the dim glare of Spago's artificial light. He noticed the many freckles on her face for the first time. Freckles even dotted her pale lips. Merlin had never seen that before.

"I'd like to be the one to help you write it," she said, getting back to her pitch.

"You don't think I could write it myself?"

"Of course. Do you want to?"

"No. I play trumpet. And I paint sometimes. But I don't write. Not even letters."

"Well then, how about it? Or maybe you'd like to see how this interview comes out first?"

"No," Merlin said, as he drank down his vodka martini in one gulp. "You're hired."

Kimberly smiled broadly. "Just like that?" Merlin realized that this was the first time he had ever seen her smile. It was very appealing; her whole face came alive. Her dimples appeared. And her thin lips, nondescript in repose, broadened considerably with her smile. It was contagious. Merlin, notorious for his frown, grinned in response.

"Just like that."

"Why?" Kimberly, relieved and surprised that it had been so easy, took another sip of her Perrier.

"Why? Because you asked. And because you are the best looking writer I know."

"Thanks," Kimberly said. "I'll take my compliments where I can get them."

"Don't you want a real drink?"

"No." Kimberly shied away from his gaze and looked down at the table. "No, thank you."

"Well, all right, if you want to be a party pooper. But anyway, I was going to say, that I have known some pretty heavy writers in my day. I knew James Baldwin. I know Alex Haley and Norman Mailer."

"I'm impressed."

"You ought to be." Merlin picked up the toothpick in his martini glass and scraped off the two olives with his teeth.

"I'm a BAD-ASS motherfucker!"

"I believe you. What happened between you and Tara Marlowe?"

"Never should have married the bitch. Is that fucking tape recorder on?"

"No."

"Good. How come we talk about me all the time? How about you?"

"What about me?" Kimberly sipped her mineral water.

"You married? Got a boy friend?"

"Was married. Divorced. I am seeing someone. But it's not serious. At least, not yet."

24

Kimberly sat at the far end of the sofa, near the corner of the tiny shack, and as distant from her father as she could get. She would have to endure this for a few hours, and then she could leave. It hadn't been so bad when she was drinking. It had been so much easier to take a long swim in the 'River of De-Nile'.

But this was her first sober Christmas since leaving home in 1968. Come to think of it, even that last Christmas she had been tripping on acid. It was also her first Christmas without Michael, now her ex-husband. Tommy, her six year old nephew leaped over to her corner to show her his latest prize, a stuffed reindeer doll, with a big, red nose.

"Look what Gramma gave me, Aunt Kimberly."

Gramma, Vivian Gates, sat smiling, in her Barcalounger at the opposite end of the room. She was large. She had put on so much weight, she could only move with great effort. She suffered from arthritis and poor circulation. She had difficulty breathing.

Kimberly picked up the reindeer to inspect him.

"Oh," she said, "this must be Rudolph, the Red-Nosed Reindeer."

"No," Tommy said, reclaiming his doll and hugging it hard.

"His name is Radar."

"Oh, I see," Kimberly said, lamely.

"And what have you got, Kim?" Kim was Tommy's older sister, older, that is, by one year. Their mother Natalie was Kimberly's younger sister and only sibling. Kimberly and Natalie had not been especially close, since Kimberly left home in 1968. In spite of, or, perhaps, because of, what they had been through together as children.

"Grandad gave me a Mr Potato Head." Kim came closer to her namesake aunt to show her the various eyes, ears, noses, hats, and mouths that Don Gates had given her.

"What you need," Don said, "is a potato to stick them in." Don got up from his chair on the far end of the sofa and went to the kitchen in search of a potato.

He was a short, skinny, wiry man. Kimberly could

remember when her parents were about the same size. Then her father had gotten skinny, perhaps it was cirrhosis, as her mother blew up like a blimp. Kimberly kept thinking of the nursery rhyme: 'Jack Sprat, he ate no fat, his wife, she ate no lean'. How did that go? Kimberly could not remember the rest of it.

"Here, Kim," Don said, handing his present to his granddaughter. His breath reeked of Jack Daniel's. "Here's a potato. Make us a face."

"Okay." Kim climbed up and sat in her aunt's lap. She began experimenting with the various eyes and ears to see what she could do to make a face that would amuse her grandfather.

Don went back to the small kitchen and poured another Jack Daniel's. It was his third. That is, the third that Kimberly had seen him pour. God knows how many he had already had before she came over.

When Kimberly used to guzzle booze daily herself, she heaped scorn on people who counted drinks. She thought of them as busybodies, goody-two-shoes, Puritan assholes, minding other people's business. But now she counted her father's drinks and wondered how long it would take him to get drunk and abusive.

She hadn't understood when she was little. Hadn't understood the relationship between the alcohol and the abuse. She just knew that sometimes her father was sweet, and sometimes he was a maniac. In a towering rage, he would pick on her for something insignificant. If she had left her tricycle or a roller skate in the driveway, he would come at her yelling.

It always started with the yelling. Then he would slap her, and she would cry. And that would make him angrier. He would slap her several times before he hit her with his fist. If she tried to run, he would take off his belt and whip her good. She had learned it was better just to stay there and take it.

Once she heard her father yelling and had hid. Don Gates had beat up Natalie instead. Kimberly had felt bad about that. Her younger sister had taken the whipping she deserved.

Deserved? Kimberly smiled bitterly as she held up a possible mouth for Mr Potato Head. Little Kim shook her head and put the mouth back in the box.

Of course, Kimberly had deserved the beatings. That's what

parents do, isn't it? They beat you up when you're bad. They punish you when you've done something wrong. But why would the same action, like accidentally knocking over a flower pot, produce hugs on one occasion and bitter blows on another?

She tried to think of something else. Some other place. Let her spirit soar. She'd not always been here. In this prison. She had been young and free once, a flower child. But her days in San Francisco blurred into a fog. She'd been stoned most of the time. She loved drugs. All kinds: marijuana, hashish, LSD, opium, cocaine, speed, downers, and, of course, booze. You name it. She had tried it all. Funny, every time she came home, it felt like she'd never left.

"What do you think of him, Aunt Kimberly?" Kim held up her finished potato face for her aunt's inspection.

"I think he's very handsome. Why don't you go show him to your father?"

Jim, Kimberly's brother-in-law, was sitting on the floor, next to a stuffed Garfield, and amid a huge pile of discarded ribbon and wrapping paper. He was trying to put together a doll house that Kimberly had given her niece for Christmas.

"Dad?" Kim stuck her creation in front of Jim's face.

"That's nice, Kim. Go show Gramma, while I try to get Barbie's house in order."

"Show me," Don said. "I gave her the fucking toy."

Oh no, Kimberly thought. Here it comes.

"Dad!" Natalie said. "Watch your language."

"I'll watch what I please," he said and got up to pour himself another Jack Daniel's.

"Behave yourself, Don," Gramma said, playing with her new radio-alarm clock that Jim and Natalie had given her.

"What do you hear from Michael, Kimberly?" Don asked, sitting back down again.

"Nothing, dad. We're divorced."

"I was reading in the *Reader's Digest* the other day about how so many divorced couples are getting back together these days."

"Well, Michael and I are not getting back together, dad."

"Well, this article said that it's the latest thing. Everybody's doing it."

"Not everybody, dad. *I'm* not doing it."

"Kimberly," Vivian said, "your father's just asking. Don't get touchy."

My father's just an asshole, Kimberly thought, as she routinely rifled through the pages of *Lonesome Dove*, the book that Jim and Natalie had just given her for Christmas.

"Are you seeing anyone special, right now?" Gramma Vivian asked.

"No, mom. I'm working and finishing up my degree in journalism at UCLA."

"Well, I'm sure there are some nice young men there."

"That's where you met Michael, wasn't it?" Don asked.

"Daddy, will you please stop talking about Michael?"

"Kimberly, you calm down, now," Vivian said.

"No. No, I won't." Kimberly stood up and gathered together her purse and her presents. "I'm sorry. But I have to go. I have an article I'm working on for *L.A. Magazine*. I need to get back to it."

"On Christmas Day?" Vivian Gates asked in disbelief.

"Yes, mom. On Christmas Day. Merry Christmas, everybody."

Kimberly was out the door, but her sister was right behind her.

"Kimberly, what's wrong?"

The tears were rolling down Kimberly's cheeks.

"I just can't sit there, Natalie, and watch him get drunk and pretend like we're the Brady Bunch or Ozzie and Harriet or something. I just can't take it."

"Kimberly, it's Christmas Day."

"Natalie, he used to beat me. Remember?"

"But that was a long time ago."

"No. Not for me, Natalie. It was yesterday. It's right now. It's today."

"Call me?"

"Sure."

Kimberly got in her green VW Rabbit and headed north toward her apartment in Mar Vista. Shit, she thought. No wonder I used to get drunk. I can't stand who I am and where I came from. Sobriety sucks. And reality is also a greatly overrated concept.

Kimberly didn't see any celebrities dining at Spago's that night — except for Merlin Black. Unless maybe the white-haired man, sitting in the corner, was Sidney Sheldon.

"Is that Sidney Sheldon, over in the corner?"

"Who?"

"Sidney Sheldon. The writer."

"I don't know. I'll go ask him."

"No!" Kimberly shrieked in a loud whisper. It was too late. Merlin walked over to the man. They chatted briefly, the man stood up, and the two of them ambled back to the table.

"Kimberly Gates," he said. "Meet Sidney Sheldon."

Kimberly gave him her hand. "Mr Sheldon, it's an honor. I think I've read everything you've written."

"Well, Miss Gates, it's a pleasure to meet you. I understand you're going to write Merlin Black's biography."

"Well, yes," Kimberly said. "Only it's more like helping him to write his own autobiography."

"I want a signed copy," Sheldon said. "A first edition."

"You've got it."

"Well, Merlin, I have to get back to my dinner companions. But it has been a wonderful experience to meet you and Miss Gates. I love your music. I've listened to your records, ever since you used to play with Charlie Parker."

"Thank you, Sid. It's been a gas."

The two men shook hands, and Sidney Sheldon went back to his own table.

"I can't believe you did that!" Kimberly said. But she was not really upset. She was so excited at the prospect of writing Merlin's autobiography that she could kiss him.

"Now, tell me about that boyfriend," Merlin said. "I bet he couldn't introduce you to famous writers like Sidney Sheldon."

"His name is Harvey Wilson."

"What does he do?"

"He's an insurance agent."

"Wow!"

"Shut up," Kimberly said. "My editor was right. You *are* impossible." The smile on her face belied her words.

"Ever date a black man?" Merlin asked.

"No."

"Prejudiced?"

"No."

"What about me? Isn't this a date?"

"No, Merlin." Kimberly said. "This is business."

"Is that why you're not drinking?"

"Yes." Again, Kimberly avoided the subject. It was her job to ferry out information about Merlin.

"What if I asked you out, Kimberly? Would you say 'yes'?"

"After we finish your autobiography. Maybe. It might get sticky otherwise. Can we order? I'm starving."

"What's wrong with sticky? Sticky is good. The best things I know are sticky."

Kimberly picked up the menu. "What looks good to you? I understand the pizza is outta-sight."

"The Kimberly looks good to me. Soft and tender and delicious to eat."

"Down, boy," Kimberly said, still considering her choices. I don't see my name on this menu."

"Well, put it down for a minute and talk to me."

Kimberly lowered the menu from her face. "Merlin, I'm hungry. Talking to you is hard work."

"Okay. Okay. Can I have one more drink first?"

"Yes. If you drink it fast."

"I always drink it fast."

"I noticed."

"What does that mean?"

"You drink too much."

"Who made you my nurse?"

"Nobody. But you act like you need one."

"Women!"

"Is that the way Tara was?"

"That's exactly the way Tara was."

"Tell me more about her."

"Can't we talk about something else?"

"Only if you let me turn on my tape recorder."

"It's a deal."

Kimberly fished the small recorder out of her purse.

"Tell me how you first came to New York and how you met Charlie Parker."

Merlin reached down to grab his two bags, as the train came to an abrupt stop. One of them was an old-fashioned carpet bag which contained his trumpet, his clean underwear, a few apples, and the only remaining sandwich. The other piece of luggage, which held most of his clothes, was more of a chest, with heavy leather straps. It did have a handle, so, with a little effort, he could carry both items at the same time.

Merlin stepped off the train and walked across the platform to the nearest flight of stairs. He felt like he was the only man in civilian dress. Every other male was either a sailor or a soldier. Merlin, who hoped the war would end before he would be eligible, was still too young for the draft.

He came to the top of the station, and his jaw dropped in open-mouthed amazement. The ceiling of Grand Central Station seemed like the vault of heaven itself. Merlin had never seen anything like it. The roof, which looked to be over ten stories high, was painted with bright gold and blue constellations — more vivid than the actual night sky itself.

Merlin moved out of the way of the most immense rush of humanity he had ever seen. He had to back up against the wall in order to find a spot where he would not be either shoved down to the floor or caught up in some violent flooding river of busy and determined people.

He had little idea of where he was or where he was going. Except he had come to New York to find Charlie Parker and to make a name for himself as a trumpet player. Leaving had been easy. There was nothing holding him back in Memphis. He wanted to get away from his mother, if not Harriet. Merlin planned to go back to Memphis and to Harriet, but he must make his reputation first.

He had to force his mouth shut and remember to breath. The main concourse was, far and away, the largest room he had ever seen. And he seemed to be the only person there who was not hurrying toward some destination, with a vengeance.

Up until this moment, he had not been afraid. Quite the opposite. He was fairly drunk on the notion of getting to the big city, finding Charlie Parker, and commencing a career that would bring him fame and fortune. His father had promised to give him $60 a month for a year, until he could get on his feet.

Gazing around the gigantic room, Merlin's eyes soon rested on the information desk at the center of Grand Central Station. So, he took a deep breath, picked up his bags, and made his way through the forest of humanity. The sounds of normal people talking in a normal tone of voice reverberated off the immense walls and came back to his ears as a screaming Tower of Babel.

"Can you tell me how to get to 52nd Street?"

"Do you see that door over there?" The skinny white man at the counter pointed toward one of the large portals.

"Yes."

"Can you read?"

"Yes." Merlin thought he had left racism behind him when he got on the train at Memphis. But he sensed that this condescending clerk assumed that all Negroes were illiterate.

"Well, what does it say?"

"It says 42nd Street."

"Can you count?"

"Yes."

"Well, then. You count off ten blocks north of here. And you'll be on 52nd Street. That's pretty easy, isn't it?"

"Yas, suh. Yo' sho' kind to us poor darkies."

"Think nothing of it. And son?"

"Yas suh?"

"You want a piece of advice?"

"Yas suh."

"Turn around and get on the next train back to whatever cottonfield you walked off of. They'll eat you alive in this town."

"Yas suh. Ah sho' does appreciate yo' hospitality."

Merlin made his way toward the 42nd Street Portal, muttering "Miserable, motherfucking, honky sonofabitch," under his breath.

If Grand Central Station was a shock, 42nd Street was even worse. As loud as the train terminal was, outside was deafening. It felt like every car in Manhattan, and at least half of them were taxi cabs, were all blowing their horns at the same time.

Merlin could not even count how many lanes of traffic there

were across the endless highway. Beale Street, at its wildest, was a country road in comparison. The skyscrapers surrounded him. He looked up and got dizzy just trying to see the top of these concrete mountains. He did not so much set a course, as he was swept up in an undercurrent of irresistible force. One could not stand still in New York. It seemed to be the only prohibition.

Merlin tried to keep his mouth shut as the stream poured past shops, theaters, museums, bars, strip joints, restaurants, and hotels. And huge, blinking neon lights of red, green, blue, and yellow. And everywhere, the blare of noise, both of people and of horns. And everywhere, the smells of food and flowers and perfume and human urine and sweat and excrement.

Finally, Merlin found himself at a huge intersection. A triangle with a small park in the middle. And all of humanity was converging on this spot. He looked up at the street sign and realized he was on Broadway — *the* Broadway, the Great White Way.

In front of him was a huge, triangular building with enormous neon lights, blinking red and white and jumping around, animated like a movie cartoon. And at the base of the sign was a rushing frieze of white letters, flashing out the world's news to the Manhattanites, too busy to stop. In too much of a hurry to read a newspaper or listen to the radio. The news said something about Hitler, and Berlin, and the end of the war in Europe.

But Merlin was too caught up in the excitement, in the swirl of action. He made his way across Broadway, past Times Square, past the statue of George M. Cohan, up 47th, up 48th. Soon he would find 52nd Street and Charlie Parker. He was practically there.

Merlin was weary of his bags, so he decided to look for a hotel. The first two hotels he approached told him that they were full up. Merlin wasn't sure if this were true or if he was being discriminated against. But the third hotel, the Century Paramount, rented him a room. It was clean, but spartan. There was no view. His window looked out on a brick wall.

Merlin put his large suitcase on the bed and began to unpack. But weariness soon overcame him. He put the suitcase away in his closet and lay down.

When he woke up, it was dark. At first, he was not sure

where he was. But then he heard the honking horns and remembered. It was night-time in New York. He was only a few blocks from 52nd Street. It was time to start looking for Charlie Parker. The New York energy began to flow. He took his trumpet case from the carpet bag, put on his coat, and walked down to the lobby of the hotel.

He felt almost at home now. He had the rhythm of the streets in his feet. And he could feel the music, jazz, his music, even before he heard it.

And then he was there. He had read all about 52nd Street, 'Swing Street', in the pages of *Down Beat* and *Metronome*. So, it felt almost like a homecoming when he saw the signs reading: 'The 21 Club', 'Mammy's Chicken Koop', 'Club Downbeat', 'Club Carousel', 'Club Samoa', and 'The Spotlite'.

The traffic crawled slowly: Hudsons, Dodges, Fords, Chevrolets, Cadillacs, Packards, but mainly yellow and black checkered taxi cabs. The pedestrians dominated, however. They were not one bit intimidated by automobiles, but crossed the street recklessly in merry, singing droves.

The self-appointed 'Mayor of 52nd Street', a local lunatic, beloved and encouraged, patrolled the area, dressed in his uniform and waving his gigantic, Groucho Marx cigar. The doormen, all up and down the street, called out loudly, as Merlin passed.

"Come one, come all. Come on in to Leon and Eddie's. Tonight we feature Sherry Britton, world famous exotic dancer. Show starts in thirty minutes."

Merlin passed by the restaurants and the strip joints. He paused only to read the names of the musicians on the billboards outside the entrances. Art Tatum was playing at Kelly's Stable. Billie Holiday was singing at the Onyx. Louis Armstrong was at the Yacht Club.

Merlin passed all these by, until he came to the Three Deuces, featuring Charlie Parker and his band. Merlin paid the cover charge. It was the first money he had spent from the sixty dollars his father had given him for his first monthly allowance. On the train, he had eaten only the food his mother had prepared for him. He put his wallet in the front pocket to make it hard for pickpockets to find it.

Inside, the bar was full of smoke and people, loudly laughing and murmuring. Merlin found a table close to the bandstand.

"What's your order?" the waiter asked.

"Oh, I don't want anything."

"There's a two drink minimum."

"Oh. Well then, I'll take gin." Merlin thought the man would ask him for an I.D., but he didn't.

"Straight gin?"

"Yeah. Straight." Merlin had only drunk alcohol once in his life, a beer, which he had not particularly liked.

"Shall I bring both drinks now?"

"Sure," Merlin said. "Bring on both drinks."

The band hit the stage. There were five musicians: drums, bass, piano, trumpet, and Charlie "Bird" Parker on alto sax. The other four really didn't matter. All eyes and all ears were on Bird. Merlin had seen him once before in Memphis with Billy Eckstine and his Orchestra, where he was so far beyond the others in the band that there was no comparison. Bird did not disappoint.

He had an amorphous face that never quite looked the same twice. This quality was exaggerated by his dramatic weight gains and losses. He was not a handsome man. But his face was round, friendly, and unthreatening. He seemed to Merlin much larger and much older than he had looked only a year earlier in Memphis. He was dressed in a loud, double-breasted, pin-striped outfit, not quite a zoot suit, but almost.

But when he stood up close to the mike and blew his horn, magic filled the smokey room. The notes flowed out in a miraculous barrage of sound. It seemed like ten men playing. Bird had more moves than most big bands. The fluttering, floating, breathless, aerial leaps of his sax left no doubt as to the origin of his nickname.

Merlin's drinks came. He took one sip of the gin and inhaled fire. He almost spat it out, but he was determined not to disgrace himself. He swallowed the gin and forced down a second gulp.

Meanwhile, Bird unceremoniously walked off the stage, leaving the rest of the band to fend for themselves. Merlin caught him by the sleeve of his coat.

"Mr Parker?"

"Yes?"

"My name's Merlin Black."

"So?"

"I have my trumpet here. I was wondering if you'd let me sit in tonight."

"What's in that glass?"

"Gin."

Bird sat down at the table and drank Merlin's second gin in a single swallow.

"How much money have you got on you?"

This was not the response Merlin was expecting. He had paid two dollars to get in and fifty cents for each drink, so he had fifty-seven dollars of his monthly allowance left. What if Bird wanted it all, just to let him play? Merlin would not be able to pay his hotel room. He would not be able to live until his father sent him his next month's allowance.

"Ten Dollars."

"Let me have it."

Merlin reached in his wallet and gave Charlie Parker a ten dollar bill.

"Thanks, kid," Bird said, sticking the bill in his pants pocket, as he got up and walked off toward the men's restroom.

He came back a few minutes later, just in time for the final chorus of the number.

When the set was over, Merlin approached Bird who was sitting with his trumpet player at a table in the corner.

"So, can I play in the next set, Mr Parker?"

"Who are you?" Bird asked. His eyes were droopy, and his pupils enormous.

"I'm Merlin Black. I just gave you ten dollars."

"Sit down, Marvin and order us all a round of drinks. Do you know Clark Terry?" Bird motioned toward the other man at the table.

"Pleased to meet you," Merlin said and motioned for the waiter.

The drinks came, and Bird again inhaled his in one swallow.

"Now, listen to me, Marvin…"

"Merlin."

"I beg your pardon?"

"My name is Merlin."

"You looks more like a Marvin to me. Wha'cha think, Clark?"

"Marvin," Clark chuckled. "Definitely, a Marvin."

"You see, Marvin, Clark Terry here is my trumpet player. The customers paid to hear Clark Terry play. That's what it says on the billboard outside: 'Clark Terry, trumpet'. Now, if I let you get up there and make a fool of yourself, you'll be making a fool of me too. You dig?"

"I won't disappoint you, Mr Parker. I promise."

"How much money you got, Marvin?"

"Ten dollars."

"Yeah? That's what you said last time."

"I promise. That's all I have. And if I give you that, I won't be able to pay my hotel bill. I won't have room or board for a month."

"What happens in a month, Marvin? Daddy gonna send you another check?"

Merlin was feeling desperate. This man was going to suck him dry and leave him penniless.

"You give me that ten dollars, and you can follow me up to Minton's in Harlem tonight. After hours, they let amateurs sit in. And if I say 'Marvin', they'll listen to Marvin. Dig?"

"Don't take the kid's money, Bird," Clark Terry said.

"All right, Clark. You always did have a soft heart. Special Intro-Ductory Offer. You rides with Bird tonight, free of charge. That is, of course, if you pay the taxi fare."

Merlin rode with Bird to the wonderful world of Harlem that he had dreamed of, all his life. Minton's Playhouse, the birthplace of be-bop, did not disappoint. It was actually more plush than some of the clubs on 52nd Street. Clean, bright, and comfortable, an abundance of seats and tables converged on a large, well-lit stage. Tablecloths and napkins broadcast that this joint had real class. And Merlin was introduced to the gods that he worshipped.

He met Dizzy Gillespie, Coleman Hawkins, Art Tatum, Lester Young, Bud Powell, and his old idol, Cootie Williams. He met Roy Eldridge, Benny Carter, Lionel Hampton, and Thelonius Monk.

The music that night eclipsed any Merlin had ever heard. But he spent the whole time worrying if Bird would let him play. And what he would do, *if* Bird let him play. How would he sound to this sarcastic, money-grabbing god and all the assembled heavenly host?

Finally, toward the end of the evening, Bird walked up to

the microphone. "Gentlemen," he said. The cigarette smoke in Minton's, by now, was so thick Merlin could barely see the stage.

"There's a new talent in our midst right here in Harlem tonight." Several people chuckled. "It gives me great pleasure to introduce to you that child prodigy, the unbelievably eloquent boy wizard: Marvin from Memphis."

There was more laughter than applause. Merlin shook, sweat breaking out on his forehead. He felt both exhausted and petrified with fear. He could barely stand up. Somehow, he managed to get his trumpet out of the case. He made his way to the stage, but tripped on the step. Lionel Hampton, who was sitting on the front row, laughed out loud. Merlin recovered his balance and made his way over to the mike. The stage light scorched. He felt sweat form on his entire body and feared he might pass out.

It seemed like an hour before anything happened, but, finally, the drummer began to pound out a furious beat. It almost deafened him. Merlin wanted to run away. To go back to Memphis. But, trembling, he put the trumpet to his lips and blew. The sound squeaked out, barely audible. He looked out at the audience. He thought they were all laughing at him. He blew again. This time the sound blurted out, louder but off-key.

Merlin looked down into the faces of Cootie Williams and Dizzy Gillespie. Bathed in the eerie yellow of the stage light, they looked strange, unreal. Creatures from another planet. And they were laughing at him.

Suddenly, from some subterranean burst of adrenalin, he discovered the strength that had temporarily abandoned him. He blew again. This time he found both the key and the tempo. He could not, at first, make the wild fluttering improvisations of his heroes. But he played. And, as he played, his confidence grew. He remembered all those years of practicing and listening. He began to improvise, hitting high notes and low. He lifted his trumpet high up in the air and blew toward the ceiling. He heard a few hands clapping.

But, just as he began to feel good, the drummer stopped. Bird jumped on stage and put his arm around Merlin.

"Let's hear it," he said. "Marvin from Memphis!"

***

When that long night finally ended, about 3am, and Merlin began to walk back to the hotel from Harlem, he was ecstatic. His first night in New York and he had met some of the giants of jazz. He had played for them, and they had listened. Merlin knew that the years of practicing and discipline, the risk he had taken in moving to New York, the fears he had in leaving behind all that was safe; all of these sacrifices would pay off.

He could conquer the world. Anything was possible. Merlin never questioned his decision to walk back to his hotel room from Harlem. He knew nothing yet of subways, and he could not spend any more money on taxis. He did not know how he was going to make it through the month, as it was.

He had a very long walk ahead of him, but, for a while, he floated above the cement, high on life's infinite possibilities.

He walked down Central Park West and even darted inside the park, near the Lake to take a peak. As he was coming back out to the street, he saw a woman standing in the shadows.

"Hey, boy, you want a good time?" she asked, as he walked by. She was a black woman with straight "processed" hair, wearing a very tight-fitting, red dress.

"Naw," he said and kept walking.

She strolled beside him for a while. She had on high heels and swung her hips in an exaggerated way. She felt his thigh with her outstretched fingers.

"Come on, I'll give you a special deal. Don't you like girls?"

"Git away from me."

Merlin kept his eyes toward the front, hoping she'd go away and leave him alone. He had no intention of spending any money on a whore. She kept touching him, and he kept brushing her off. Finally, she reached down and stroked his crotch.

"Oh, I bet I know what you want. You want a blow job, don't you?"

"I tole you to leave me alone."

She stuck her hand on his crotch again and began to rub his penis.

"Come on, boy, I'll treat you right."

Merlin began to run. She ran after him and grabbed his hips from behind.

"What's the matter? You a queer?"

Merlin ran faster. She made no attempt to keep up. He turned around: she had completely disappeared.

Goddamn whore, he said to himself. Oh well, maybe next month, after I have a regular gig. After I become Bird's trumpet player. He walked another few blocks, before he reached down to pat his front pocket for his wallet and realized it was gone.

"Goddamnit!" he said out loud. "That whore done stole my money." He turned around and started racing back in the opposite direction.

After a few blocks, he realized it was futile. The whore, who probably wasn't really a whore at all, but just a pickpocket, was long gone. He turned south again, the tears forming in his eyes. He was angrier at himself than he was at the woman. He should have known better. He should have known that he was being robbed. What the fuck was he going to do now?

A car rushed by and he heard a woman's voice scream something out, apparently at him. The car raced on past him, up the otherwise dark and empty street. He heard something plop down on the sidewalk.

He ran up to it and picked it up. It was his wallet. Empty. All his money for the next month — gone. Only then, was he able to place together the words the woman in the car had screamed at him. She had said: "Welcome to New York — sucker."

"You remember the time Bird was so fucked-up he pissed in the phone booth?" Merlin asked.

"Yeah," Peter Pollard said, bringing Merlin a vodka and Kimberly a *Perrier*. "I was never quite sure whether he did it out of spite, or because he really didn't know where he was."

Peter's house in the Hollywood Hills looked down on the Sunset Strip. At night, the view from his window exploded into a symphony of lights. But it was still only late afternoon.

Peter and Merlin had been friends since the late 40's. Peter had come to New York from San Francisco, hoping to play jazz. The best conservatory for be-bop at the time was the strip of nightclubs along 52nd Street. Like Merlin, Peter wanted to study with Dizzy Gillespie, Charlie Parker, and Thelonius Monk.

Peter loved music. It was his life. He had no great need for fame or riches. As long as he played music with the best, he was content. And that he had done.

Within the first few years in New York, Peter came to understand that he himself was no prodigy. He was competent. He could play almost any musical instrument. He could sound like Thelonius Monk on the piano and like Charlie Parker on the alto sax. What he could not do was sound like Peter Pollard. He was not an original.

Still Peter understood every aspect of the music business. He had a formal background. He could read and write music. He could arrange. He was even good at the business end, setting up gigs, haggling over salaries, and dealing with difficult club owners.

He always seemed calm. He never raised his voice, and no one ever saw him angry. Perhaps it was for that reason, the reason that he was the polar opposite of the volatile Merlin Black, that the two men had gotten along so well and for so long.

It did not take Peter long either to figure out that Merlin *was* an original. Merlin learned from Dizzy Gillespie, and he also learned from older trumpet players, Louis Armstrong and Cootie Williams among others. But Merlin did not play like any of his mentors. He soon forged his own style. A lean

41

and yet lyrical style that was instantaneously recognizable as Merlin's sound.

The moment that Peter first recognized that sound was the moment which sealed his fate. He was willing to work at Merlin's side, anonymously if need be, just to witness his friend's inspiration and to be a part of Merlin's gift to the world.

Peter was truly color blind. He always sought to work with the best talent in jazz, and most of that talent was black. He never made an issue of race, never looked down his nose, or assumed airs. He genuinely did not seem to notice. He had lived with Merlin and other black musicians, and they had lived with him, on terms of equality, at a time when that was uncommon. His wife Maria was black, and they named their son Merlin.

It was ironic too, because in his younger years Peter looked the perfect redneck. He had a farmer's, skinny body and a large, prominent adam's apple. When his hair was brown and short, you'd have thought that he'd just fallen off the turnip truck.

He looked less like a redneck now, because his hair was silver and long in the back. He was balding in the front, a fact which he strove to hide by wearing loud bandannas around the top of his head. The one he had on at the moment was white and red.

Merlin, sitting on Peter's sofa next to Kimberly, took the vodka from his host. Peter handed the *Perrier* to Kimberly, who accepted it with a smile.

"Yeah," Peter said. "Bird was a genius. But he was impossible to work with. He'd never talk about the music he played. I don't think he knew how to articulate it. Do you, Merlin?"

"Naw. I've been trying to describe those days to Kimberly. The be-bop days. How new and shocking Bird's music was then. But the dude was so fucked-up on smack all the time, that, even if he could've explained, he'd of been incoherent."

"Yeah," Peter said, going back into his kitchen to pour himself a glass of wine. "How's the interview going?"

"The interview's completed," Kimberly shouted, so that Peter could hear her in the kitchen.

"Right," Merlin said. "The interview is finished. Now we

write the autobiography."

"The autobiography?" Peter said, as he walked back into the room with his glass of wine.

"What do you think about that?" Merlin asked. He drained his glass and put it on the carpet, next to the sofa.

"I think it's great," Peter chuckled, as he adjusted his sagging bandanna with his left hand, "as long as you don't tell the truth."

"You don't have anything to worry about," Merlin said. "I'm the one who's been a bad boy."

The front door opened. A middle-aged black woman, large but attractive, and an adolescent boy walked in. The boy, who looked something like Peter but with darker skin, was carrying a trumpet case.

"Kimberly," Peter said, "this is my wife — Maria."

"Hi," Maria said, stepping up and extending her hand.

Kimberly shook hands with Maria. "Hello, Maria. Glad to meet you."

"You guys seen the *Times* today? *Calendar* section?" Maria asked.

"No," Peter said. "Why?"

Kimberly walked over to the boy. "Hi," she said, "my name's Kimberly."

"Hi," the boy said, putting down his trumpet case.

"I'm sorry, Kimberly. This is our son, Merlin."

"Merlin!" Kimberly said.

"Yeah," the older Merlin said. "He was named after me."

"No kidding," Kimberly said, smiling back at him. "I thought maybe it was some other Merlin."

"Anyway," Maria said, "you guys made the paper today."

"Really!" Peter said. "What does it say?"

"Well, we take the paper," Maria said. "Whad'ya do with it? I read it in the beauty parlor."

"I think I left it in the bathroom," Peter said, leaving the room to look for it.

"So, you play the trumpet?" Kimberly asked little Merlin.

"Yes ma'am."

"Just like your namesake?"

"Oh, I don't know, ma'am. I'm not that good yet."

"I don't know, kid," Merlin chuckled. "I haven't really played in five years. You might have caught up with me."

43

"Here it is," Peter said, coming back into the living room with the newspaper. "Let's see: 'Jazz Legend Stages Comeback' by Morris Leonard."

"Leonard!" Merlin said. "That ignorant honky!"

Kimberly sat back down on the sofa.

" 'Jazz legend Merlin "the Wizard" Black'," Peter continued, " 'will play publicly for the first time in nearly five years, August 23, at the Hollywood Bowl. Rumors are rampant about the feisty and controversial trumpet player who disappeared from the public's eye five years ago after being hospitalized, subsequent to an apparent suicide attempt'."

"Shit!" Merlin said. "Skip to the good part."

"O. K. 'The legend of Merlin "the Wizard" Black, also known as "the Prince of Darkness", has grown steadily… blah, blah, blah… In 1968 traditional jazz fans and black radicals booed him off the stage of Carnegie Hall for using electronic instruments…"

Little Merlin left for his room, and his mother disappeared into the kitchen.

" '…In trying to bridge the gap between "old fashioned" jazz and contemporary rock and roll, it seemed Merlin had pleased no one. Or, as the influential jazz critic Jack Geeland, in the pages of *Down Beat* magazine quipped at the time: 'The Wizard has Fizzled: Merlin, the son of a Memphis lawyer… Attacked by feminists for calling women bitches'."

"Enough!" Merlin said, escaping over to Peter's front window.

"Wait," Peter said. "There's something in here somewhere about me. 'Mr Black has always been an outspoken critic of American racial policies… criticized both Martin Luther King and Malcolm X, as clinging to the white man's superstitions. Merlin said the black man can never be friends with the white man whose "proven agenda is enslavement and exploitation." Some find this ironic in a man who has often had white friends and associates, including'… Ah-ha! Here it is… 'his long-time arranger and companion Peter Pollard'."

"Told you — you were in there some place," Maria said, briefly popping in from the kitchen.

"Like another drink for the road, Merlin?" Peter asked.

"Sure."

"It's okay," Kimberly said. "I'm driving."

"I'll get it," Maria said. "What'ya drinking, Merlin?"

"*Stoli* on the rocks."

"Coming right up."

"Peter," Merlin said, "about those musicians of yours..."

"We're playing tonight at the Catalina Bar and Grill." Peter took the glass of vodka from his wife and handed it to Merlin. "Why don't you and Kimberly come over and hear us?"

Merlin drank off the *Stoli* quickly. "Kimberly?"

"Sure," she said. "I'm game."

"Valerie Rachel is my pianist," Peter said. "Plays like a combination of Thelonius Monk and Bill Evans. She's terrific! Then we have this young guy on sax, Jafar Ali. Plays tenor and soprano. He's great too."

"Well," Kimberly said, standing up, "if we're going tonight. I need to go home and change first."

"Where do you live, Kimberly?"

"Oh, I have an apartment over in Mar Vista."

"Well," Merlin said, shaking Peter's hand, "we'll see you tonight. Thanks for everything."

"Bye," Maria called out. "Nice to meet you, Kimberly."

Merlin and Kimberly walked outside to Kimberly's green VW Rabbit. She took the wheel and headed south for the Santa Monica Freeway.

"What time shall I pick you up, tonight?" Merlin asked.

"Oh, no," she said, as they descended a steep hill. "I'll pick you up. I'm not riding with you, the way you drink."

"I could get a taxi or a limo."

"It's all right," she said. "Save it for next time. I don't mind driving." She remained silent for a while, as she looked for the freeway on-ramp. Finally, she said: "Tell me about your sons, Merlin."

He turned to examine her attractive profile, the serious expression, the freckles, and the thin lips. "The two kids were different from the very first," he said. "Gene, the older, was obedient. You could tell he had his problems. That Harriet had told him bad things about me. But he didn't let on. He acted like a soldier in the army: stood at attention and didn't speak until spoken to. Benjamin was more playful, when he was younger. Seemed more carefree. But he got bitter as he got older. He got into drugs in the 60's and couldn't stop. He kept on taking drugs. Like me, I guess."

"Where are you going?" Harriet asked, accusingly. She stirred the beans on the top of the stove. The smells of beans and greens and pot roast permeated their little, spartan, third floor apartment in Harlem. They spent most of their time in the kitchen/living-room combination, which was all they had, anyway, except for a small bedroom and a microscopic bath with poor plumbing.

"I have to go downtown to practise with the guys," Merlin said. "We have a recording date tomorrow."

Gene and Benjamin played checkers on the floor. They wore knickers and pullover sweaters. Gene was a year older and never let Benjamin forget it. He beat him every time they played checkers or any other game. Still, Benjamin did not give up. He idolized Gene but firmly believed that, if he kept trying, someday he would catch up.

"You coming back for dinner?" Harriet asked.

"No."

"You coming back tonight at all?"

"If I get through in time."

Harriet took off her apron, turned around, and looked at Merlin. "You're seeing another woman, aren't you?"

"No, Harriet." Merlin took his overcoat from the coat rack and put it on. "I'm too busy working to have time to be courting other women."

Harriet threw the apron on the kitchen table and sat down.

"Yeah, you be workin' all the time but never bring home any money. How's that?"

"Harriet," Merlin said, picking up his trumpet case. "I make enough to feed you and the kids. Don't I?"

"You make a whole lot more. What you do with it?"

"I ain't got time to argue, woman. I'm late as it is."

"What am I'm supposed to do if your father gets in tonight?"

"Feed him."

Merlin walked out of the apartment and down the stairs. He couldn't wait to get outside. The air on 124th Street smelled like freedom. Harriet was driving him crazy. Besides, he was beginning to feel funky.

He hailed a cab.

"Do you know the Oxford Hotel on 110th between Seventh and Lenox?"

"Sure," the cab driver said. "Hop in."

Bird was staying with Art Mclean, the bass player in their band. His room looked even worse than Merlin's apartment. The bed was naked of sheets or blankets. Beer bottles, sandwich wrappers, and bread crumbs littered the floor.

"Marvin!" Bird said, when Merlin walked through the door. "Delighted to see you, my good man."

Bird sat on the bare mattress of the bed, drinking out of a large jar of cheap, red wine. He unsnapped the top button of his shirt and pulled the tie knot away from his throat. His loud, wrinkled, broadly striped suit was stained with large, purple wine spots.

"Where's Art?" Merlin asked, taking off his coat.

"Trying to score. You holding?"

"No," Merlin said, sitting down in a straight chair. "I was hoping you'd have some shit on you."

"Dry as a bone," Bird said. "Would you like some vino?"

"Okay." Merlin stood up, took the large bottle from Bird, tilted it to his mouth, and drank deeply. "You gonna be able to play tomorrow?" he asked Bird, who looked totally wasted.

"Sure," Bird said, taking the wine jar back from Merlin. "Don't I always?"

"Usually," Merlin said.

Art, a large man with dark skin and heavy eyebrows, came back to the room about an hour later. He had only been able to score three caps. Bird immediately took off his coat and his tie. He squeezed the tie around his arm to make a vein.

"You shootin', Merlin?" Art asked.

"No. I'm just snorting."

"You better go ahead and shoot. It's pretty dry out there. It may take a while before we score again." Merlin found the belt of Art's brown bathrobe, hanging on the railing of the bed. He tied it around his upper arm. He watched as Art stuck the needle in his vein.

***

Later, Merlin walked home along Lenox Avenue. It's almost

Christmas, he thought. He felt much better. He wouldn't get hooked on this stuff. He wouldn't allow himself. It was just a kick. Something to pass the time. He smelled chestnuts, cooking on a street grill and coffee, drifting outside from a diner.

He heard Benjamin crying, even before he climbed to the second floor.

"What's wrong with that baby?"

Harriet was sitting at the kitchen listening to *Amos and Andy* on the radio.

"I can't do nothing with him," she said. "He won't stop."

"Where's Gene?"

"He's already in bed. It's late, in case you didn't know."

Merlin picked Benjamin up and held him in his arms. He thought Benjamin looked more like him, while Gene favored his mother.

"What's the matter with you?" Merlin asked the boy as he gently rocked him up and down. Benjamin's cry mellowed into a whimper. Merlin put him to bed.

Someone knocked on the door. Merlin opened it and stared into the eyes of his father, Edgar Black. He hadn't changed. He looked tall and stern. He still wore his hair short and sported a thin whisper of a moustache under his long, pointed nose.

Edgar Black stored his suitcase and took off his overcoat. Harriet got up to fix some coffee.

"Is something wrong, daddy?" Merlin asked. "You look worried." He still felt high, although his father's presence sobered him up considerably. All three sat around the table holding cups of hot coffee.

"It's your mother," Edgar Black said. "She's not well."

"What's wrong?" Merlin asked.

"I had to put her in the hospital. She's... well, confused."

"Crazy as a bessy bug," Harriet said.

"Shut up, Harriet! Merlin stared holes through her. "That's my mama you're talking about."

"Sorry."

"Well," Edgar Black said, looking down at his coffee. "I had to tell you in person, and I wanted to see you. I know we've sorta lost contact. But I hope now, we can be closer."

Merlin wasn't entirely surprised. He had known, for a long time, that his mother was unstable.

Merlin felt animated as he removed the keys from the ignition of his blood-red Jaguar, which he had just parked in the rear of the Hollywood Bowl. He pulled his trumpet case up from behind his seat and then bounced over behind the car and opened the other door for Kimberly. He could not remember the last time he had opened a door for a woman. It seemed part of a world that had disappeared along with tuxedos, 78 records, and elevator operators. You're almost afraid to open a door for a bitch these days, he thought, afraid she'll slap you in the face and call you a "chauvinist pig" or something worse. I'll have to stop using that word. Kimberly certainly isn't a bitch. I'll call her a lady, he thought, although that's probably not politically correct either.

But Merlin didn't care today. Today he was dauntless. He felt like he was waking up from a long nightmare, a nightmare that began the terrible day he heard about Cheryl's death and that only really ended two weeks ago when Kimberly Gates had walked through his heavily locked back door.

Anyway, no matter what the feminists' catalogue of forbidden words for the day might be, Merlin mused again, Kimberly was definitely a lady, whether she liked the term or not. And she looked particularly pretty today. Her long, frizzy hair seemed orange in comparison to the crimson scarf on her head. She put the scarf on because Merlin had driven the Jaguar with the top down. Kimberly also wore a soft, cottony, summer dress of pastel blue, which gave her a sort of willowy, windblown look.

He felt good about being around her. He found himself taking extra pains with his appearance, wearing a blazer and his hairpiece, which he hadn't bothered with in months. Merlin was frankly flattered that this good looking woman wanted to write his life's story. He had brought her here to the Hollywood Bowl, ostensibly to try out the acoustics, but really to impress her.

"Have you ever played here before?" she asked, as they stepped up on the stage and stared out at an ocean of chairs: from the society boxes in the front to the cement bleachers in the back.

49

"Yeah once. Back in '65, I think it was."

"Where are we having lunch today?" Kimberly asked, while gazing up at the famous shell with its gigantic rows of semi-circular curves.

"Food! That's all you ever think about, woman. It's a wonder you ain't fat."

"I think you promised to take me to Chasen's sometime."

"I will take you to Chasen's sometime. But not today. Today, we're going to Aunt Kizzy's in Marina del Rey for some soul food. If you want to know the real Merlin, and what my music is all about, then you gotta understand soul food."

"Okay," Kimberly said, smiling. "Whatever you say." She removed the red scarf from her head and put it in her black, leather handbag. Then she shook out her hair by bending forward first and then flopping it back into place.

Merlin thought that was sexy. He had no idea how she got those frizzy curls in her hair, but he liked them. It couldn't be natural, he thought. She must have to put her hair up in curlers every night, like they used to do back in the 50's. Surely nobody's hair comes that way naturally. Kinky, yes. Frizzy, no.

He had never noticed that kind of frizzy hair before. And then, one day, it was everywhere he looked. At least, every third woman in L.A. had frizzy hair. Where had they learned it? Who told them to start wearing their hair that way all of a sudden? Probably in one of those secret meetings, with no men allowed, where they got together to decide what words were no longer politically correct. They also made a plea for frizzy hair, beginning on March the third, 1990. What a vast secret network women must have! It makes the CIA look like fucking amateurs.

"Now, you go up there about half way," he said.

"You want me to jump off this stage and climb half way to the top?"

"Bingo!" Merlin put his trumpet case down on the stage.

"That's more exercise than I've had all week."

"Gotta stay in shape, if you're gonna write my autobiography, lady." Merlin's expression went from cocky to insecure in a second, as he realized what he had just said. "Is it all right if I call you 'lady'?"

" 'Lady's good. Certainly better than 'bitch'. I noticed you haven't called me that all day. Thanks!"

"S'okay. Now get yo' ass outta here."

"Yes, sir." Kimberly smiled her broad smile again. She dropped her purse on the spot, sat on the edge of the stage, and pushed herself down into the orchestra pit. Then she climbed out of the pit and walked past the front rows which were divided into boxes for the benefactors and subscribers. Merlin watched her as she scurried up about thirty more rows. Her ass was a little broad, but fleshy and shapely. Outstanding for a forty year old, white woman.

Kimberly cupped her hands to her mouth. "How's this?"

"Super!" Merlin put his trumpet to his mouth and blew one long, high note. "How's that?"

"Beautiful," Kimberly called. "Play 'Stranger in Paradise'."

Merlin thought about this old song from the musical *Kismet*, one of his most enduring hits over the years. He knew that his chops were seriously out of shape. It would take him a week of disciplined practise before he could play anything as complex as "Stranger in Paradise."

"I don't play that honky music any more."

"Well, play something. Anything."

Merlin put the trumpet to his lips and played the opening of Prince's song, "Little Red Corvette." He blew several sour notes before he stopped.

"Come on back down, Kimberly."

Kimberly took a last look at the huge, curved shell and crooked, brown hill behind it. She stared too at the lonely, brooding figure on the stage. Merlin held his trumpet and gazed, slightly stoop-shouldered, down at the orchestra pit.

She had known his music most of her life and loved it, especially those numbers that were lyrical and tender. It was difficult to reconcile those sweet melodies with this man who seemed so bitter and angry. But then she realized that the beauty and the tenderness were part of him too. Perhaps the best part. What he could not say in words, he blew through his trumpet. And that was his real message to the world.

"That was great," she said, after she had worked her way back down to the stage.

"It wasn't, but thanks for saying so."

He reached out his hand to help her back onto the platform. As soon as she returned to the stage and regained her balance, he dropped her hand but grabbed her around the

51

waist and kissed her. She pulled back, not angry but surprised. She wanted this but not yet. She didn't want anything to jeopardize her chances of gaining a reputation as a writer, by co-authoring his autobiography.

Merlin noticed her reluctance.

"Are you angry at me?" he asked.

"No."

"Do you think I'm ugly?"

"No, you're handsome."

"What then?"

"I'm just not ready. Can we discuss this later over lunch?"

They were both embarrassed. Merlin felt like a teenager on his first date. Silently, they found their way back to the car without looking at each other.

"Why did we do that?" Kimberly asked, as they got back in Merlin's Jaguar.

"The kiss?"

"No. No. I mean why did we come here to the Bowl."

"Acoustics." Merlin stuck the key in the ignition and started up the car.

Kimberly pulled her compact tape recorder out of her purse. "May I turn it on?" she asked.

"In the car?" Merlin thrust the gear shift into reverse and turned around to make sure no one was behind him.

"I won't, if you don't want me to." Kimberly jerked the red scarf out of her purse too and threw it around her head.

"Naw, go ahead." Merlin lurched into traffic. He drove south on La Brea, headed toward the San Diego freeway.

Kimberly clicked on the tape recorder.

"How do you define honky music, Merlin?"

"Music that ain't got no soul."

"Do you hate all white people, Merlin?"

"No," he said, smiling in her direction. "Not all of 'em. There's a few I don't hate."

"Tell me about Cheryl, your wife."

"Wha-cha want to know."

"The article in the *L.A. Times* said you tried to kill yourself when you found out she was dead. Is that true?"

"Naw. I just got a little careless. That's all."

Merlin fought through the pain and the darkness and the numbness to focus his unwilling mind on the loud, obscene buzzing of his telephone. He forced his naked body out of the brown sheets of his waterbed and stumbled around the large room, looking for the source of the noise, which in his hungover condition seemed like a torture out of the Spanish Inquisition.

He had been in his new Malibu house less than a month and was easily disoriented. Then he remembered that the phone was on the table next to his bed. He picked up the receiver.

"Merlin, why haven't you signed those divorce papers yet?" asked the angry, shrill voice on the other end of the phone.

"Who the fuck is this?" Merlin struggled to gain consciousness against the overwhelming misery in his head. For a split second, in his demented state, he thought it might be Cheryl. He had waited for her call for twenty years.

"Who'd be asking you about divorce? How many wives you got anyway?"

"Tara?"

"Bingo!" Tara Marlowe couldn't intimidate Merlin, although she came closer to it than anyone else he had ever known. He didn't care if she had won an Oscar, a Tony, and an Emmy. He remembered her when she was a nobody. Merlin had known her for over twenty years, since before his divorce from Cheryl. In fact, Tara had been the primary cause of that divorce.

Merlin married her several years later. It had been a mistake. Worse, a disaster for both Merlin and Tara, and it had soon degenerated into bitter acrimony.

"I don't feel too good, just now, Tara. Can we talk about this some other time?"

"My days of nursing you are over, asshole! You'd better get professional help. If you keep popping pills and drinking all the time, you're gonna kill yourself. Do you want to die, Merlin?"

"Right now, Tara? If you don't hang up and stop bugging

53

me, the answer is 'yes'."

"Well, I can't help you any more."

"Who's asking you to?"

"You. In your usual passive-aggressive way."

"Fuck you."

"Well, if you'd tried that a couple of times, maybe you wouldn't need all those drugs and booze."

"Shit, Tara, I'm not up to this. I just got out of bed."

"Yeah, how many bimbos are there with you?"

"None, Tara. I'm by myself." Merlin looked back at his rumpled bed to make certain that he wasn't lying.

"Merlin, look. Will you sign the divorce papers today and send them to my lawyer like I asked you to, a month ago?"

"Yes."

"Promise?"

"Yes."

"You've still got them, don't you?"

"Yes, goddamn it, Tara. I'll sign the fucking papers and get them out today. Now, will you get off my case?"

Merlin hung up the phone, because he knew he had to throw up and soon. He despised the necessity, but there was no use trying to avoid it. Vomiting had become part of his morning ritual. Although it was no longer morning. It was already late afternoon.

He felt it coming, welling up inside. Merlin just managed to get the toilet seat up before the pale broth from his stomach heaved itself up and out. One more time, he knew he would have to retch again. He managed to get most of the vomit into the toilet. He wiped up the rest with a towel which he then threw into a wicker hamper. The cleaning woman will be in tomorrow, he thought.

Next he brushed his teeth and tried, as usual, not to look at himself in the mirror. Not me, he thought. That pathetic old man is not Merlin Black. Somebody was playing a hideous practical joke on him, and he wasn't buying it for a second. Temporarily, he found himself in the *Twilight Zone*, but soon he would be back to normal. Both the way he looked and the way he felt. The horror would end, and he could resume his normal life.

But until then, he would continue his "morning" routine. He went back into the master bedroom. On the night stand,

54

next to the lamp and the telephone was a silver monogrammed cylinder and a thin, deliberate trail of white powder. He got down on his knees, and, hands shaking, held the cylinder to his right nostril. He snorted up the line of cocaine, the powder stinging all the way down.

Merlin did not necessarily brush his teeth before going to sleep. But there was one bedtime duty he never forgot. He always made certain to leave out a line of coke each night, for fear he wouldn't be able to make it through the next "morning." This kneeling down by his bed every night and every morning reminded him of something he had nearly forgotten — kneeling down to pray, when he was a kid growing up in Memphis. And perhaps the comparison was not so far-fetched.

As the coke began to kick in, a little, Merlin stood up and walked into his luminous white-tiled kitchen. The thought of food was not appealing, but Merlin knew he had to eat something.

He forced down a cold English muffin, while waiting for his coffee water to boil. He couldn't even wait until it was bubbling, just hot enough to melt the freeze-dried crystals that he sprinkled into a cup. He poured the cup half full of the hot water, plopped an ice cube into the cup and topped it off with vodka.

Merlin drank this concoction, and, in a a few minutes, he began to come alive. He went back to the master bedroom, sat on the side of the waterbed, and rang his agent on the tan, push-button phone. Barry Franklin, a thin, middle-aged black man, had been Merlin's agent for almost thirty years.

"Barry? This is Merlin Black."

"Merlin, this had better not be bad news," came the cautious, bass voice on the other end.

"Barry, I'm not going to make it to Chicago."

"Merlin, do you know how many gigs you've broken in the last six months?"

"I can't help it, Barry. I'm sick."

"Yeah, I'd be sick, too, if I took as many drugs as you."

"Barry, do you know where Cheryl is?"

"Cheryl? Your ex-wife Cheryl?"

"Yes, Barry. Who else?"

"Merlin, how would I know where your ex-wife is? You've

been divorced for twenty years. What about Tara? Are you guys breaking up or what?"

"The bitch woke me up this morning. No, Barry, I've been thinking about Cheryl a lot lately. I really loved her. I made a big mistake, letting her go."

Merlin suddenly flashed on the first time he had met Cheryl James, back in 1954, shortly before he kicked heroin and came into his own as a jazz musician. He had just put together the quintet that was going to make him a household name.

Cheryl was nineteen, a featured dancer with the American Ballet Theater, one of the first black women in the company. And beautiful! She had a round face with delicious dimples, light, smooth, cafe-au-lait skin, huge, brown eyes: meltingly, sweet, and a slim, supple, dancer's body.

Their time together had coincided with Merlin's greatest popularity. It was the only happy time in his life. He couldn't even remember why he had ever let her go. Technically, of course, she had left him. But only after he had callously neglected her.

"Merlin," Barry Franklin said. "It's a little late to be talking about Cheryl. Don't you think?"

"Did she remarry? Is she living with somebody? Barry, tell me."

"Merlin, I don't know. The last I heard she was back in St. Louis with her mother. But that was years ago. We don't exactly travel in the same circles."

"How would I go about finding her?"

"Merlin, you and Cheryl broke up over twenty years ago. I'm worried about you. Do you want me to call your shrink?"

"No, goddamn it , Barry. I want you to call Cheryl. I need her."

"Merlin, you must be out of your fucking mind, man. First of all, I'm not your secretary. Second of all, I *am* your agent. And as your agent, I have to tell you, buddy, you're flushing your career straight down the toilet. There are maybe ten clubs in America that will not book you any more. The word is out: Merlin Black never shows up. Merlin Black is so strung out he can't stand up and hold his trumpet at the same time."

"Barry, don't do this to me, man."

"Who's doing what to whom, Merlin? I book you into one of the few clubs that will still take you, and you cancel on me."

"I need a rest, Barry. I'm not well."

"You're gonna get a long rest, pal. This will kill it. Whose gonna ever believe me now when I say Merlin Black will show up for a gig?"

"Barry, can we talk about this later?"

"Later is now, pal. I mean it. If you're not on that plane for Chicago tonight, you had better start looking for a new agent!"

Merlin winced as Barry slammed down the receiver in his ear. He pushed down the hang-up button with his forefinger and immediately called information.

"What city, please?"

"St. Louis, Missouri."

The woman gave Merlin the number, and he called the St. Louis operator.

"Do you have a listing for a Mrs Martha James or a Cheryl James?"

"I show no such listing," came the pert voice on the other end.

"Well, how about a Cheryl Black then?"

"Sorry sir."

"Shit!"

"I beg your pardon, sir."

"Nothing, operator. Thank you for looking."

"You're welcome sir."

Merlin put down the receiver and propelled himself toward his creamy-tan tiled bathroom. He opened the glass doors to his shower and turned on the water. He stood a long time inside, as the hot water relaxed his tired body. He lathered up all over and had just begun to rinse off when he heard the intercom buzzer ring.

Merlin toweled off and grabbed a dark-blue, silk bathrobe with a red flower pattern. He pushed in the appropriate button on his intercom system.

"Yes? Who is it?"

"It's us," the decidedly female voice replied. "The two girls that you requested. From the agency."

"What agency?" For a moment, Merlin genuinely had no idea what this was about.

"Nora's Modeling and Escort Agency. Nora said you left a standing order to send two girls up every week at this time."

"Oh, right. *That* agency."

Merlin clicked open the Schlage double-bolt and the three other locks, and then opened his back door. There on his back porch were two brassy, young women — one white and one black — both wearing six-inch, spiked heels, miniskirts, and skimpy blouses.

The black woman, who was chewing gum loudly and shifting her weight restlessly from one hip to the other, said: "Hi, Merlin. I'm Tinkerbell."

"Oh yeah," Merlin said. "And who's your friend here, Snow White?"

"Yeah sure," Tinkerbell said, still shifting and chewing. "Whatever ya like. Can we come in, or what?"

"Come in. Come in. By all means, come in."

"We brought the videos like you said to." Tinkerbell had African, "corn-row" braids and a full, generous body.

"Great." Merlin, who now remembered placing this order, led the two hookers into the living room and asked them to have a seat.

"Would you like a drink?"

"Yeah," Tinkerbell said. "Sure. Got any tequila?"

"One tequila coming up. How about you, Snow White?"

Snow White was a short, thin blond with a mole on her right cheek.

"Could I have a wine spritzer, please?" she asked timidly.

"Look, honey, I ain't no bartender. Could you keep it simple?"

"Right. Could I have a white wine, then?"

"Can do. Now, if you girls would just make yourselves at home for a few minutes, I need to make a telephone call, before we get started."

Merlin fixed the drinks and poured himself a vodka. Then he called Peter Pollard.

"Peter?"

"Merlin! What's up?"

"Would you call the boys and tell them that we're not going to Chicago?"

"Sure, Merlin. But I know they'll be disappointed."

"Can't make it, Peter. Barry's making all kinds of noises, but I'm just not up to it."

"I understand, Merlin. Agents always make noises. That's

what we pay them for." After a short pause, he asked: "Is it anything you want to talk about?"

"Well, no, Peter. But there is something I want to ask you. Do you know anything about my ex-wife, Cheryl?"

"No, Merlin. Not really. You want me to make some inquiries?"

"Would you?"

"Sure. I'll get back to you."

"I've got two whores over here, Pete. You want to join me for a frolic?"

"Sounds like fun, Merlin. But I'm afraid Maria wouldn't understand."

"Aw shit, man! You always was pussy-whipped."

"Well, that's true, Merlin," Peter said, laughing at the same time. "But if you got to be whipped, can you think of a better instrument?"

"Peter, you're a real motherfucker! And the best friend I ever had. You know that, don't you?"

"Now, Merlin. You're not gonna get sappy on me, are you?"

"No. No. Thanks, man."

"All right, Merlin. Catch you later."

"Okay, girls," Merlin said, putting down the phone.

"Showtime! Would you like another drink first? Or maybe a little nose candy?"

"Sure, man," Tinkerbell said. "It's yo' party. You name the dance."

"Well, let's have one more drink and move into the bedroom." Merlin poured Snow White more wine and Tinkerbell more tequila. He stuck one of the X-rated movies in the VCR and fast-forwarded through the opening episode.

"What you got in mind, Merlin? You want a blow job performed simultaneously by two beautiful girls? Does that turn you on?"

"How come you do all the talking, Tink?" Merlin asked, still studying the TV screen, his finger on the fast-forward button. "Snow White mute or something?"

"No, she's just shy. Ain't you, Snow White?"

"Right." Snow White said, sipping her white wine.

"Come here, girls. Let me show you something." The girls stood up and looked at the TV. It was a scene of two women performing oral sex on each other. They were lying on their sides, each with their head in the other one's crotch.

"That's what I want you to do. Can you do that?"

"Sure, we can do that. Can't we, Snow White?"

"Right," Snow White said.

"But we'd rather please you than each other."

"You'd please me just fine, if you'd please each other."

Merlin brought the vodka bottle into the bedroom and sat down to watch the two women make love to each other. They both had good bodies, and Merlin was amused that Snow White, who seldom said more than: "Right," seemed the more aggressive lover of the two. He drank freely, straight from the bottle, and found himself becoming increasingly aroused.

He wasn't sure why he got off on watching two women making love. He certainly didn't want to watch two men fucking or sucking each other, but two women, that was exciting. Especially when one was white and the other was black. Merlin's interest in kinky sex was a relatively recent phenomenon. Unambiguously heterosexual, nonetheless, Merlin had been, if anything, austere over the years.

Finally, after about twenty minutes of voyeurism, and half a bottle of vodka, Merlin felt sufficiently "turned on" to join the hookers. He took off his bathrobe, crawled right down the middle of the bed, and snuggled between them.

"Okay, Snow, baby. I think I'm about ready for that blow job." Snow White knew her business well. Without missing a beat, she turned her attention to Merlin's crotch. She licked his scrotum, like the best X-rated movie actress, and began to suck his already engorged penis, deeply and expertly.

Merlin turned toward Tinkerbell, whose breasts he began to fondle. She kissed him warmly and rubbed her fingers around his nipples. I'm not the only magician in the room, he thought, as the girls worked their magic on him, and he quickly was transported toward orgasm.

Normally, at such a moment, he would not have answered a ringing phone. Whatever impulse led him to do it this time, he could not later remember. Probably, he was not thinking at all; at least, not about who might be on the other end of the receiver.

"Yes? Who is it?"

"Merlin? This is Peter Pollard. Are you sitting down?"

"I'm lying down. Is that good enough? Oh shit! Snow White, baby! That feels good. Don't stop." Snow White, holding his cock with one hand, smiled and looked up at him for a second, before attacking him once more, plunging down his shaft and sucking most of him deep within her mouth.

"What did you say, Merlin? I didn't hear that."

"Make it quick, Peter. I'm occupied."

"Oh, okay. Cheryl's dead. I located her mother. Cheryl took an overdose of sleeping pills about two weeks ago."

"Oh, God!" Merlin said, as his sperm jerked out of him and into Snow White's mouth. "Oh, God! No!"

Merlin slammed down the receiver and screamed: "Get out! Get out! Goddamn it, get the fuck out of this house!"

"What's the matter, baby?" Tinkerbell asked. "Wasn't that a good blow job?"

"Get out!" Merlin shouted, and then he jumped out of bed. He grabbed the almost-empty bottle of vodka and threw it against the wall, the glass flying around the room. The two women, alarmed, gathered their clothes and made for the door.

"Do you want us back next week?" Tinkerbell asked.

"Get the fuck out, now!" Merlin shrieked, like a soul in hell, and then fell to the floor. He heard the front door slam as he moaned aloud and began to roll around, in anguish. He grabbed his knees and rolled from right to left in small arcs, until his naked back came in contact with the first shard of glass.

The physical pain felt good and seemed to take his mind off the pain in his head. Merlin could not articulate the meaning of his pain. He could not say, "I feel terrible, because Cheryl is dead." He could not say, "I feel terrible because I cheated on her and spent all these years without her." He only felt a loss beyond measuring, a bottomless emptiness and a regret beyond redemption.

He let go of his knees and turned his entire body across the floor, covered with pieces of the shattered vodka bottle. He welcomed each new wound as deliverance from his anguish, as penance for his guilt. The room was soon soaked with his blood. Peter called back. Merlin did not answer.

"Did you blame yourself for Cheryl's death?"

Kimberly sat in her favorite brown leather chair in Merlin's living room. She wore a sky-blue colored blouse with a button-down collar and khaki bermuda shorts. She had become more informal and more relaxed in his presence. Merlin wore his black silk pyjama bottoms and a white sweat shirt. He paced up and down the room, with the usual glass of vodka in his hand.

"Yes."

"Why?"

"If I'd been there more often. If I hadn't fooled around on her."

Merlin refilled his glass from the bottle of *Stoli* on the bar.

"Do you experience a lot of guilt, Merlin?" Kimberly felt great tenderness for him. She was not certain, if she had fallen in love with the subject of her book or with the man himself.

"Believe it or not, I blame myself for everything. For Cheryl. For Harriet. For Benjamin. For my mother."

"You blame yourself for your mother's mental illness?"

"Yes." Merlin walked over to the large plate glass window and looked out. It was early evening, unusually clear for Los Angeles. The stars writhed with unaccustomed brightness. "I carry around a lot of guilt. Don't you?"

"Yes," Kimberly said. "But then I'm Catholic."

"I thought all you Catholics could get absolved of your guilt."

"A common Protestant misconception. We get absolved from sin. Not guilt."

Kimberly turned around and gazed at the dark sky.

"Oh, God, it's late! I have to go." She put her note pad away and began to gather together her things.

"Are you mad at me for trying to kiss you yesterday?"

"You didn't *try* to kiss me. You kissed me. And, no, I'm not mad at you."

"I love you, Kimberly."

"I already told you I'm seeing someone. And besides..."

"You said it wasn't serious."

"And besides, I don't think it's appropriate, while I'm

writing your book. It's like a conflict of interest to…"

"Walk outside with me for just a minute. Will you do that?"

"Okay. But then I really have to go."

Merlin guided her through the sliding glass door, onto the porch, and down the steps into the sand. They walked away from the lights of the house, and Merlin pointed up at the firmament.

"It's beautiful!" Kimberly said.

"You ever think about what it all means?"

"Sure," she said.

"Well, I guess, as a good Catholic…"

"I'm a Catholic," she said. "Nobody said anything about good."

"But you believe in God?"

Kimberly looked up. The moon was almost full; the stars, incandescent. The heavens formed a magnificent, dark dome to the boundless Pacific. "I think it's almost arrogant to believe that this is all an accident. What do you think?"

"Well," Merlin said. "I figure there are basically two possibilities. One, the universe has always been and will last forever. It's eternal, infinite, and constantly expanding. There was no creation. No beginning. No Big Bang."

"Yeah?" Kimberly said. She slipped off her sandals, and she and Merlin began to stroll down the beach toward the lights of Santa Monica.

"But," Merlin insisted. "If there was no creation, then that means there was no Creator. No God. No meaning. Life is simply an accident. Time doesn't exist; it's a human illusion. Truth, justice, beauty, shit like that, are simply statistical majorities. Love is no more than a twitch in the groin, a biological trick to promote reproduction. My life, your life, Martin Luther King's life, the entire human race is of no more cosmic significance than a bug that I accidently step on when I walk down Wilshire Boulevard."

"Or?" Kimberly asked, as she skipped down to meet the foam of an incoming wave.

"Or," Merlin said, as he caught up with her. "And this is what I want to believe. There was a Big Bang, a Creation. Time exists. And that opens up the possibility for a Creator, although, I've never had any personal experience of any kind of god or anything like that. It does open up the possibility of

63

meaning in the universe. Then there's value to life, in general, and human life in particular."

Kimberly stared back at him in open-mouthed wonder. She had never heard him talk like this before. "I didn't know you knew so much about science."

"I read," Merlin said. "Here's the downside. If the universe had a beginning, then it also has an end. If there was a Big Bang, there will also be a Big Crunch. After the Big Crunch, the universe will cease to expand and begin to contract."

"Says who?" Kimberly stopped, kneeled down, and picked up a sea shell. She looked at it, washed it off in the salt water, and put it in the right pocket of her shorts. They continued strolling down the beach.

"Stephen Hawkind. People like that. It stands to reason. As the universe contracts, everything is played out in reverse. What was torn apart will come back together. Explosions will implode, and the stars come closer. Everything will be again. But opposite. Backwards. And, at some point..." Merlin grabbed her left hand, and Kimberly stopped walking and turned to face him. "And at some point, billions of years from now, you and I, Kimberly, we'll meet again."

"Really?" she said, beaming.

"Yeah," he continued, smiling also. "But next time, I'll be younger than you. You'll be the older one. And you'll want me, as much as I want you now."

"Really?" she said again, leaning toward him.

"Yeah." His head floated down to her mouth, and his lips touched hers. Kimberly threw her sandals on the sand. She put her arms around him and kissed him back. It was a long kiss followed by several shorter ones.

"So," she said, finally. "I better be nice to you now, so you'll show pity on me, next time around?"

"Exactly."

"Nice try, Merlin, but I gotta go." She pulled away from him and bent over to pick up her sandals. "Tomorrow, I want you to tell me more about Benjamin."

"My son, Benjamin?"

"Of course, Merlin. Who else?"

She raced, hips swaying, through the sand of the beach toward the lights of Merlin's house. Smiling, he watched her recede into the night.

Merlin felt profoundly uncomfortable. Not just because of his geographical location in rural Mississippi, surrounded by hostile white people. But also because of his mental location, surrounded by hostile black people, his own people: Harriet and their two sons. He wished that Tara had come with him, but hadn't thought it appropriate to bring his new wife to meet the mother of his children.

"You want some more coffee?" Harriet asked him. No longer skinny, she had filled out to the point that she looked just like her mother, Mrs Loomis.

"Sure," Merlin said, holding out his cup for her to pour more steaming, brown liquid into it.

All four of them sat in Harriet's dining room, looking out the large front window at the small lake. Harriet called the place, that Merlin had bought for her, a farm, but it looked to Merlin more like a swamp. As far as he knew, her worthless husband Matt never planted any crops. He supposedly worked at a garage in Hernando, but Merlin footed all the bills.

"How about you, Gene?" Harriet said, offering the coffee to her oldest son.

"Sure, mom." Gene looked uncomfortable too. He had Harriet's oval head but the stern look and the square jaw of his grandfather, the recently deceased Edgar Black. A freshman at Harvard Law School, he sat in the rustic rocking chair wearing a gray Brooks Brothers' suit and a red and black silk tie.

Merlin thought Gene was a little overdressed, but wouldn't say anything. Especially since Benjamin looked like a clown out of the circus. He wore a brightly-colored, purple and green dashiki, sandals, and a yellow bandanna over his long, Afro hair-style. Merlin had always favored Benjamin, perhaps because he looked more like *him*, and Gene reminded Merlin of Harriet and his father. But Merlin was peeved at Benjamin for dropping out of Stanford in order to devote all his time and energy to the sanitation strike.

Merlin believed in the cause. He had come down south to march in a demonstration in support of the striking sanitation workers in Memphis. He had already donated a good bit of money to the strike. This particular march was being led by Martin Luther King. Merlin had ambivalent feelings about King. On the one hand, he knew that King was an effective leader and orator. But on the other, Merlin was uncomfortable with the religious aspect of the movement. He felt that Christianity had been one of the tools that the white man had used to keep the black man down. He had made a few enemies by stating this opinion in public.

The strike, opposed by the white, racist mayor, Henry Loeb, had become the cause of the day and the center, for the moment, of the struggle for black equality in America. As a native of Memphis and an advocate of racial equality, Merlin felt that he should take a stand and participate directly. There was nothing unduly religious, he thought, about poor people wanting enough food on their tables to keep them from starving to death.

But he wanted Benjamin to make something of his life. Merlin had sent him to the best and most expensive schools in the country. He did not want him to throw away his opportunities, working for garbage collectors in Memphis. On top of that, Merlin noticed certain troublesome signs. Benjamin kept twitching and scratching, and his eyes were dilated.

"Why you want to live down here in Mississippi, Harriet?" he asked.

"Why you ask? You don't think it's pretty down here?" Harriet poured coffee into Benjamin's outstretched cup.

"Ain't you afraid of the Ku Klux Klan?" Merlin asked.

Harriet looked at him as if surprised. "I ain't afraid of no Ku Klux Klan. Course I ain't the one going up to Memphis to demonstrate either."

"The Klan lay a finger on *my* mama, and they'll have me to answer to," Benjamin said.

"I'm sure the Grand Wizard's trembling in his boots right now," Gene said.

"Now boys," Harriet said, just before she disappeared into her kitchen with the empty coffee pot.

"Benjamin, why don't you ride up to Memphis with me?" Merlin asked.

"Why should I?" Benjamin said.

"Because I want to talk to you. That's why."

"All right," Benjamin said. "But I have to meet with some

brothers at the Clayborn Temple before the march."

"The Invaders," Gene said, putting his empty coffee cup down on the floor.

"The Invaders? Who are they?" Merlin asked.

"A gang of punk delinquents," Gene said.

"They are not," Benjamin said. "They're a Black Power group."

Harriet came back into the living room. "You boys better get started, if you're going to get to the march on time. Don't want to keep the Reverend Doctor Martin Luther King waiting. And don't forget your coats. It's cold outside."

"I'll meet you at the cemetery." Gene said, as he got into his red Oldsmobile.

"Right," Merlin said. "We'll meet you there."

Merlin shivered and buttoned his camel-brown overcoat, before opening the car door. It had been an unusually cold March in the Memphis area. It was actually colder here than it had been in New York. This demonstration had been postponed from an earlier date on account of an unprecedented blizzard that had dropped sixteen inches of snow on the city of Memphis.

Merlin slipped into the driver's side of the blue Ford that he and Tara had rented at the airport. He followed Gene out to the main road, hoping Benjamin would say something. He didn't. He just sat, slumped in the right seat of the car, looking gloomy and irritated.

It was only about a thirty minute drive to Memphis, so Merlin felt compelled to initiate the conversation.

"Tell me about the strike," he said. "I mean, I've read about it in the New York papers and all. But you've been here. What's it been like?"

"Want some weed?" Benjamin asked, pulling a joint out of his coat pocket.

"Sure," Merlin said.

Benjamin lit the marijuana cigarette with a lighter that he also had in his coat, inhaled, and passed the joint over to his father. Merlin took a toke and handed it back.

"Well," Benjamin began. "A couple of the workers got killed in a garbage compressor. And then 'The Man' refused to pay the brothers their salary, just 'cause it rained. So, in February, they walked out. T.O. Jones is the union organizer for AFSCME. But at first there wasn't a whole lot of support. Here, you want some more of this?" Benjamin handed the joint back to his father.

"So then, the preachers got involved?" Merlin asked.

"Yeah. Reverend Lawson organized the black community, and we started daily marches to City Hall."

"This is about dead," Merlin said.

"Okay," Benjamin said. He took the lit end of the joint and threw it in his mouth, paused, and swallowed it. "I love the roach, man. That's the best part. Here, take this for later." Benjamin gave his father a new, unlit marijuana cigarette.

As they crossed the state line into Tennessee, Merlin breathed a sigh of relief.

"So what happened next?"

"So," Benjamin said. "The honky, racist mayor Henry Loeb slapped an injunction on us — not to march any more. That's when Rev. Lawson called up his old friend Martin Luther King. He was supposed to be here last week, but it snowed."

"I know. I was planning on coming down."

"You mind if I turn on your radio, man?"

"No," Merlin said. "Go ahead."

Benjamin turned the radio on and fiddled with the dial until he found Otis Redding singing "Dock of the Bay."

"Otis!" Benjamin said, as he began to move his arms and head to the beat. "Far out! I guess you heard about him dying, back in December?"

"Yeah, I heard. It took his death to get him the kind of recognition he's deserved for years. A hit song now that it's too late to do him any good."

Merlin admired the blackness of Otis Redding's music. It spoke to the hip, young ghetto kids. The very audience Merlin wanted to reach with his Jazz Fusion. That acoustic shit's too white, he thought. To get to the black youth, you gotta have a screaming, electric guitar and a funky bass. Like the guys playing behind Otis. Yeah, they got the sound.

"Listen, Benjamin, I'm playing Carnegie Hall next month. You want to come up and hear me?"

"Naw," Benjamin said, still rocking to the sound of Otis. "That music's for old people."

"But I'm doing something new. I'm using an electric guitar and other rock and roll instruments."

"It's still jazz. That's some boring shit, man. Listen, I don't have time for this cemetery bit. I have to meet with the brothers. Can you just let me off at the Clayborn Temple?"

"Yeah, sure," Merlin said, clearly disappointed by his son's refusal. "Where will you meet us?"

"Pull over, right here," Benjamin said. "I'll meet you here at the temple. Okay?"

On an impulse, Merlin grabbed his son's arm and pulled up the sleeve of his dashiki. Benjamin had needle tracks from above his elbow all the way down to his wrist.

"You're a junkie," Merlin gasped.

"What do you know about it, old man?"

"I know a lot about it. I've been there. I can help you."

"Go to hell, old man," Benjamin said, opening the door and jumping out of the car. "And get off my case. Who the fuck do you think you are? My father? If so, where have you been all my life? I hate you." Benjamin slammed the car door shut and stalked off toward the church, where a crowd had already gathered.

**

Merlin picked Tara up at the Lorraine Motel. Not yet the world famous actress she would become, Tara Marlowe's beauty alone could stop traffic. The soft but distinctive features of her face, the light, creamy-brown skin, flawless complexion, and willowy figure all conspired to give her the classic appearance of a queen.

"Did Benjamin go with Gene?" she asked, as soon as she slid into the passenger side of the car.

"No," Merlin said.

"What's wrong?" Tara read Merlin's mood without difficulty.

"I think if I cut over to Beale, I can get to the cemetery without getting into the demonstration traffic."

The blue Ford cruised down the famous street, past the moribund honky tonks, once the spawning-ground for celebrated entertainers from Robert Johnson to Elvis Presley, past the statue of W.C. Handy, "Father of the Blues," and past the Peabody Hotel, renowned for its marching ducks.

"You and Benjamin had a fight?"

"Sort of."

They met Gene in the parking lot of the Memphis Memorial Park. Tara, who had met Gene a year earlier, embraced him quietly. The three of them then walked over to the grave site, which stood at the top of a small, green knoll under an oak tree.

Merlin stared down at the inscription on his mother's tombstone:

> *Sarah Black*
> *1905-1953*
> *Wife And Mother*
> *Beloved By Both*
> *Husband And Son.*

When his mother died in 1953, Merlin had been in the pit of Hell itself. A strung-out junkie, he had performed only to make enough money to score. He lived to get high, and he had degraded himself in ways that made him shudder to think. He had pimped, stolen, cheated, and lied. He had betrayed everyone who got close to him, and he had left behind a legacy of hostility and distrust.

He had lost his cabaret card in New York City and spent most of his time playing the Lighthouse in Hermosa Beach and several lesser joints in Hollywood. He would have died had he not stumbled, quite literally, into Cheryl. Now she was gone too. But maybe not forever. Maybe they could still get together some day.

Merlin shivered and stuck his hands in the pockets of his camel-brown overcoat. His gaze moved over to his father's tombstone.

> *Edgar Black*
> *1901-1967*
> *Father And Husband*
> *A Leader Who*
> *Fought For His People.*

His father had been dead less than a year. Merlin had intended to go to that funeral. He and Tara had actually boarded a plane at La Guardia. The plane, which was to take them to his father's funeral in Memphis, had been delayed. Engine trouble, the captain said. That was enough for Merlin.

"You go on," he had said to Tara. "I have to get off."

"Why?" Tara asked, clearly exasperated at Merlin's erratic behavior.

"I'm superstitious about shit like this." That was all he had said. He then got off the plane. Tara had had to go to the funeral alone and explain that Merlin was not feeling well.

Now Merlin walked over to Gene and put his arm around him.

"Your grandfather was a good man," he said. "Stern, but good."

"I know, dad," Gene said.

"I'm sorry..." Merlin paused. He had a catch in his throat and tears in the corner of his eyes. "I'm sorry, I've not done better by you boys."

Gene turned around and embraced his father.

"Dad, you've supported me. Put a roof over my head. Sent me to the best schools in the country. I know you couldn't always be there. But, I'm proud of you. You should see my friends faces, when I tell them that Merlin Black is my father."

The two men held on to each other, and Merlin patted Gene's back.

"Thanks, son," he said. "I appreciate that."

They walked back down to the car.

"Can you come with us?" Tara asked.

"No, they won't let me leave my car here. It's just a couple of blocks. I'll meet you at the march."

Merlin and Tara waved goodbye and got back in the rented, blue Ford. They drove from the cemetery to the Clayborn Temple on Hernando Street, where the march was to begin. Merlin turned on the car radio. Again, Otis Redding's warm and gravelly voice crooned "Sitting On The Dock Of The Bay" through the radio speaker. Merlin thought about Benjamin and what he had said. He pulled the joint that Benjamin had given him out of his coat pocket and lit it with the lighter in the dashboard of the car.

As soon as Tara smelled the strong, dirty-sock odor of the marijuana cigarette, she turned to Merlin in shock.

"Merlin Black! You get rid of that thing, right this minute."

"Fuck you!" Merlin said, sucking the smoke deep into his lungs.

"We're going to a public demonstration led by the Reverend Martin Luther King at a church, and you smoking that awful stuff. Put it out!"

"No."

"Okay. Then, stop this car, and I'll get out."

Merlin inhaled deeply one more time and flicked the cigarette out of his window.

"You gonna die of a heart attack, woman. You're uptight twenty-four hours a day."

Tara, who was dressed in a mini-skirted, plaid suit and a fur coat, looked over at Merlin again with boundless irritation.

"And you're the most impossible man I ever met. I'm sorry I married you."

"Well, we can sure fix that. You want a divorce?"

"Merlin, you behave, now. I don't want you to make a spectacle of yourself today. There's gonna be all kinds of people here. Important people. Harry Belafonte and his wife, for sure. Maybe others."

"People who can help your acting career?" Merlin smirked.

"Yes. And what's wrong with that?"

"Nothing."

Merlin looked out the side window of the car, silently fuming. All over town he saw signs, saying "Loeb's Barbecue," and "Loeb's Laundry and Cleaners." The Loeb who owned these establishments was the mayor's brother, but it gave the impression that the family owned the town. Merlin had direct experience with Memphis whites. He knew the racism of the city, and how deeply it ran. He remembered being beat up for no reason other than the color of his skin.

He parked, then he and Tara walked over to the Clayborn Temple, home of the African Methodist Episcopal Church. Although they were late, the march had not begun. There were quite a few people milling around with signs. Some read: 'I *Am* A Man'. Others: 'Justice/Unity', and 'End Dismal Working Conditions Now'.

Merlin went up to one of the parade marshals who was wearing a white arm band.

"What's going on?" he asked.

"Dr. King's plane has been delayed," the marshall said. "But he should be here directly."

The crowd was predominantly black, but there were a few

white people there, ministers and students mainly. Most of the men wore hats, and everyone wore coats. It was getting close to noon, but it was still quite chilly. Finally, the marshals started organizing the people into lines.

Merlin was given a sign that read: 'End Racism Now'. He could probably have gone to the front of the march, had he identified himself, but he preferred to remain anonymous. Gene caught up with them.

"Get ready," he said. "I think we're going to start."

"Have you seem Benjamin?" Merlin asked.

"No," Gene said. "I'm a little worried about him and his friends, the Invaders. There's been some loose talk about violence."

The line began to move slowly. From their position next to the Clayborn Temple, they could see the marchers way ahead of them. Merlin had been in demonstrations before, but nothing like this. This one, six thousand strong, looked like the Exodus from Egypt in the movie *The Ten Commandments*. It was not an orderly crowd; there were no rows or lines, as in most demonstrations. Instead, wide gaps and spaces alternated with other spots, where participants were densely bunched and crowded. In many places, people spilled out, over onto the sidewalks.

Merlin, Tara, and Gene were near the back as the line crawled forward at a snail's pace. The crowd stretched up a hill toward Main Street. It was noisy. A dull roar of voices. A Tower of Babel with few words distinguishable.

Their pace quickened. They actually began to march. Merlin clasped Tara with his right hand and held the sign with his left. He looked up toward the Memphis skyline. There were several landmarks, familiar from his youth. The Union Planter's National Bank with its ubiquitous "UP" logo, displayed prominently on a large signboard. The Peabody Hotel, the famous Memphis institution, where the ducks marched daily through the lobby and bathed in the fountain. The doors of the Peabody had been closed to blacks the whole time Merlin had lived here, even though it was only two blocks away from Beale Street, the heart of black Memphis.

They filed through a run-down section of the city. Many of the stores were closed, because most of the owners were participants. They passed a few clothing stores, music stores, an Esso gas station, and a shabby motel.

Even though the sound level was already high, Merlin noticed a sudden change. At first, the noise stopped. Then there was a collective shriek from the front of the march.

"What was that?" Merlin asked.

"I don't know," Tara said. "But I don't like it."

"Something's happened," Gene said.

There was another loud groan from near the front of the line. And then occurred the most astonishing thing Merlin had ever witnessed. The huge crowd, the Exodus from Egypt, began to turn in ripples. First, the front of the line, but then successive rows, until the entire procession had reversed itself, turned round in horror and begun to rush down in their direction.

Merlin felt like a man on a beach. He had been staring at a calm sea, when out of nowhere, an enormous tidal wave materialized and smashed down, all around him. If it had not been terrible, it would have been beautiful.

"Let's get out of here," Tara said.

But Merlin could not look away. He stood, transfixed by the power of a sight beyond imagination. Most people around him were fleeing: some back into the Clayborn Temple; others as far away as they could run. A few brave, if not foolhardy photographers were snapping away for all they were worth. They knew that these pictures would sell to *Time*, *Newsweek*, and papers all over the world. The unthinkable had happened: a march led by Martin Luther King had turned violent.

Tara and Gene were gone. Merlin could not turn away from the Medusa's head of a wild mob, rushing down on him like an avalanche.

He backed up slowly, still watching. But what actually had happened? Teenagers rushed around him. Some were carrying their own, home-made signs which read: 'Damn Mayor Loeb — Black Power Is Here'. Most of them shouted. Merlin heard words like "Black Power!" and "Honky pig!"

Then he heard something different. At first, he thought it was a shotgun blast. But then he realized it was something else. Black kids, high school students, had taken the protest signs off their sticks and used the sticks to smash windows. They were breaking into stores. They were looting. Merlin saw boys and girls, climbing out of shattered, storefront windows, carrying

74

away shirts, pants, coats, radios, and television sets.

Suddenly, everything became clear. At the top of the hill, Merlin saw what had caused the panic and rout. Policemen, hundreds of them appeared in full riot gear. They were wearing gas masks and spraying the marchers with mace.

But that was not all. They were beating them with billy clubs and shoving them in the stomach with rifle butts. The mace fumes were beginning to find their way to Merlin's end of the hill. At last, he turned around ready to leave. Ready to find Tara and Gene.

But, as he turned around, he saw Benjamin, headed toward a music store. Benjamin's stick had already been stripped of its sign. Merlin couldn't let him do this. He loved him. He would not allow him to wreck his life. He didn't stop to think. He ran. Benjamin had made his way to the store window.

"Stop!" Merlin yelled.

Benjamin turned around to look at his father. Good, Merlin thought, maybe I've stopped him. But still he ran. As he came within a few feet of him, Benjamin turned around, and, with a powerful swing, shattered the glass. Merlin felt the shards whiz by his head. Benjamin was inside the display window, about to grab a red, electric guitar.

Merlin made one final lunge toward him, but it was too late. He heard the deafening shot. He saw the blood spurt from Benjamin's back. He caught the body of his youngest son as it fell, lifeless, into his arms.

"Do you feel responsible for Benjamin's death?" Dr. Russell Dover asked.

Merlin stared at the psychiatrist who sat directly across from him in this small office. He was a serious looking, middle-aged Caucasian with white, receding hair and deep facial wrinkles that appeared as if they were cut from marble. In fact the whole head might have come from Mt. Rushmore, except for the large, bulbous nose that always reminded Merlin of W.C. Fields. How incongruous, Merlin thought, like putting Groucho Marx glasses and eyebrows on George Washington.

"Yes."

"Why?"

"If I'd been there more, when he was growing up. Maybe, he wouldn't have gotten strung out. Maybe he wouldn't have broken that window."

"But you approved of his taking part in the garbage strike and the demonstration led by Dr. King?"

"Yes, of course."

"And Gene?"

"I don't think Gene ever forgave me for Benjamin's death."

"Why is it," Dr. Dover began again, after consulting his notes. "Why is it, Merlin, that you never talk about your mother. You've said a lot about your father — how overbearing he was, and unsympathetic. But what was your mother like? I think you said she was an alcoholic?"

"That's right, Doc. She drank like a fucking fish."

"Was she loving and forgiving or hard and judgmental like your father?"

"Well, she was..." Merlin never talked about his mother, because he didn't want to talk about her. He didn't want to think about her either. The thought of Sarah Black made him intensely uncomfortable.

"Well, you know she died in a mental institution."

"Yes, you told me that, Merlin. That was after you left home, I believe."

"Yes. 1953. I was on heroin at the time. I didn't even go home for the funeral."

"How did that make you feel?"

Merlin felt *now* like a butterfly, pinned and wriggling.

"How the fuck do you think it made me feel, Doc? *Terrible*."

"Is that why you never talk about it? Because it makes you feel bad."

"Yes."

"Well, sometimes Merlin, we have to face our fears. We have to go ahead and just FEEL terrible. These memories won't go away just because you are not thinking about them consciously."

Merlin didn't say anything. He just gazed at Dr. Dover. He felt bad enough without actually having to work at it. He thought, instead, of Kimberly. How beautiful she was. How much he looked forward to their next session. It had become the center of his life. Not the prospect of a book about himself. Just the joy of being with her.

"You've talked a lot about your anger, Merlin. Where do you think that's coming from?"

"I get pissed off easily."

"Why?"

"I don't know. You're the expert. Maybe it's because I just have bad luck and keep bumping into assholes." Merlin paused. "Tara used to piss me off a lot. She really knew how to get my goat. That's when things began to go wrong for me. Back around 1968."

"You drink too much, Merlin Black," Tara Marlowe said, just as he rear-ended his burgundy Triumph TR-3 into the fender of the yellow taxi cab in front of him.

"Shut the fuck up!" he roared.

They had just come from their Upper East Side apartment and were on their way to Carnegie Hall where Merlin had a gig in little over an hour. They were both dressed in formal attire. Tara looked great, as usual. She wore a black evening dress, which complimented her short, straight, black hair, and light creamy-brown skin. She had soft features but a sharp tongue.

Merlin had been trying to concentrate on the upcoming concert, the riskiest move yet of his entire career, but his mind was clouded with grief and rage over the recent death of his son. I'm gonna unleash my new, electronic sound for the first time, he'd been thinking, just before the accident. I'll start the concert, as usual, with some standard numbers, played by the acoustic quintet. But in the second half, I'll bring on rock and roll musicians with electronic instruments, to play unfamiliar and as yet unrecorded, music. My old fans might not like it.

Tara's comment and the shock of the impact with the taxi cab brought Merlin out of his thoughts.

"Don't talk to me that way," she said. "I'm not a punch bag, like your first wife. Did you use to talk to Cheryl like that?"

"Yeah, all the time."

"Well, no wonder she left you then."

Merlin got out of the car to inspect the damage, which was considerable. Both cars had taken a beating, but the cab, whose rear fender was barely hanging on, had taken the worst of it. The taxi cab driver, a heavy, square-shaped man, was visibly shaken.

"This is going to cost you plenty, Mr Negro."

"Shut the fuck up, Mr Polack!"

"You dant tell me 'shut the folk up'! And you dant call me no folking Polack either. I'm Ukrainian!"

"I don't give a shit what flavor honky you are. You're still a goddamn honky. Why did you stop so fast?"

"I stop so fast, because folking car in front of me stop so fast. Why you tail-gate me?"

"I've half a mind to just coldcock you right now, you miserable Polack!"

Tara pulled Merlin back into the car. "Merlin, don't do this. Not tonight. This is about Benjamin. I know you're upset, but don't let this guy ruin your big night."

The Ukrainian was beating on Merlin's window. "Come on out now, Mr Bigass Black. I show you who's going to folking coldcut who."

Merlin rolled down the window.

" 'Coldcock', you ignorant Polack! Not 'coldcut'. That's something you put on a sandwich."

The Ukrainian cab driver spat a healthy wad of ugly moisture right in Merlin's eye. Merlin did not hesitate long enough to wipe the spit away. He pushed the door open with all his might. He forced it open with such speed and power that it knocked the cab driver down on the pavement. Just as Merlin jumped out of his car and onto the prostrate body with the intent to beat the Ukrainian unmercifully, the recently arrived policeman pulled him off.

"Whoa, there fellow. What's the problem?"

"This man just spat in my face," Merlin said.

"He assaulted me, officer," the cab driver said, standing up and brushing himself off. "You saw him, didn't you?"

"These cars are blocking traffic," the tall, thin policeman said. "Do you think you could pull them over to the curb?"

The policeman led Merlin over to the sidewalk, while his assistant and the cab driver moved the cars out of the way.

"If he insists on making an assault charge, I'm afraid, I'll have to take you to the station," the policeman said to Merlin.

"You're damn right, I insist!" the Ukranian shouted.

"May I see your driver's license?" the policeman asked.

Merlin fumbled around in his pockets until he found his wallet. The policeman took the driver's license and began to copy down the information.

"Is this your car, Mr Black?"

"What the fuck? Are you going to accuse me of stealing the car now?"

"Merlin," Tara said. "Be nice, now. Yes officer, this is Mr Black's car."

"Have you been drinking, Mr Black?"

"Say, what?"

"Have you been consuming alcoholic beverages?"

"We had one drink at his apartment before we left," Tara said. "But I can assure you we are not intoxicated."

"Well, I'm afraid you're going to have to come down to the station."

"Goddamn fascist pig!" Merlin muttered.

"Shut up, Merlin," Tara said. "Officer, I don't think you understand. This is Merlin Black, the famous jazz musician. You've heard of him, right?"

"No ma'am."

"Folking troublemaking agitator!" the cab driver said.

"Shut the fuck up!" Merlin said.

"Shut up! The both of ya!" the policeman said.

"You *have* heard of Carnegie Hall, haven't you officer?" Tara continued.

"Of course."

"Merlin is the leader of the group that's playing there tonight. In…" Tara checked her watch. "In less than fifteen minutes. Now, if he doesn't show up, why, with the tense political situation these days, and all… His fans just might riot. Now, you wouldn't want to be the cause of a riot at Carnegie Hall. Would you, officer?" Tara, the consummate actress, smiled at the policeman and batted her long eyelashes in a most seductive way.

"No, ma'am."

"Then, why don't you just give us a little ticket. And then we'll park the car and take a cab the rest of the way. I assure you, Merlin Black is not going to leave the country. And I can tell you, as an eyewitness, this beastly cab driver provoked him terribly."

"All right, Miss. We'll try it your way. But if he pops off one more time, I'm running him in. Riot or no riot."

"Oh, thank you, officer." Tara stepped back and whispered in Merlin's ear. "If you open your mouth, Merlin Black. And I mean one time. I will beat the living daylights out of you. And that's not a threat; it's a promise."

Merlin mumbled to himself and turned around. He walked to the rear of the car and opened the trunk.

"What are you doing?" the policeman asked, in a tone of voice that showed that he was clearly alarmed.

"Folking anarchist has a tommy gun!" the cab driver

shouted.

Merlin threw his hands straight up in a gesture of both surrender and exasperation. "I just want to get my horn out the car. Is that a crime?"

"Merlin," Tara said. "We have to park the car at the Lincoln Center. Just leave the trumpet where it is."

Merlin slammed the trunk shut and folded his arms. He simmered like a volcano on the verge of eruption.

***

"I need a drink," he said later as they were walking down Broadway, after having dropped the car off at the Lincoln Center parking lot.

"Not now," Tara said. "Wait till we get to Carnegie Hall. I don't want that policeman to get another shot at you."

Merlin abruptly stopped and faced Tara. The simmering volcano spilled over. "You don't want! You don't want! Who gave you the power to order me around like I was a goddamn infant?"

"Merlin Black, you ungrateful bastard! If it weren't for me you'd be in jail right now."

"Fuck you!" Merlin stormed inside Felix's Broadway Pub, slammed his trumpet case on the bar and ordered a double vodka, straight up.

"Feel better now?" Tara asked when he came back outside.

"Yes."

"Good. I hailed us a cab. Get in. We're already a half hour late."

"Fucking cab driver better not be Ukrainian," Merlin said as he opened the back door for Tara.

"I wonder who they're picketing?" Tara asked, as they approached Carnegie Hall. The demonstrators, mostly young, black males, were marching in a circle around the entrance to the music hall. Arrayed in various 60's attire: Afros, dashikis, tie-dyed shirts, blue jean jackets, and bell-bottomed pants, they were chanting and carrying signs which read: 'Merlin is an Uncle Tom', 'Jazz is Black/Rock is White', 'Merlin is Selling Out Our Black Heritage', and 'Merlin is a Tool of the White Establishment'.

"What's this shit?" Merlin shouted out, as he emerged

from the cab.

"That's what we want to know, Merlin," one of the young demonstrators, with an unusually large Afro, said. "How come you playin' white music? Do you need the money that bad?"

"You ain't even heard the music yet!" Merlin was incredulous. He was used to being called an angry, young black. No one had ever called him an 'Uncle Tom' before.

"Play our music, man," called one of the other demonstrators. "Leave that white shit to the Beatles."

Merlin swung around to confront his new antagonist, who happened to be the one carrying the 'Uncle Tom' sign. "You ever hear of James Brown or Jimi Hendrix?"

"You ever hear of John Coltrane or Charles Mingus?" called out another.

"Hear of 'em," Merlin shouted, wincing at the memory of his recently deceased friend, John Coltrane. "I taught those motherfuckers every sound they knew."

"Merlin," Tara said, pushing him into the small, wood-panelled door of the Artists' Entrance. "Leave those boys alone, now. They're just kids."

"I don't believe this shit!" Merlin walked down the dark hall, beside the main auditorium, which led to the backstage entrance.

The musicians were all waiting for him. There were two distinct groups: his old quintet and the new electronic instrumentalists. They were not difficult to tell apart. The older musicians of the acoustic quintet were all dressed, like Merlin, in tuxedos. The younger group wore dashikis and bell-bottomed jeans like the protesters outside. The older musicians all sat rigidly in folding chairs, while the younger ones were mostly standing around the coffee pot drinking from white, styrofoam cups.

"I want you to play real good tonight," Merlin said. "Tonight's a special event. You know Martin Luther King has been in my hometown of Memphis, trying to help the black sanitation workers on strike down there. Well, the proceeds from tonight's gig is going to help the cause. We're gonna donate our salaries to the men that are out of work and to their families who don't have no food on their tables."

"Shit!" said Art McLean, the electronic bass player, after a short pause.

" 'Shit'?" Merlin said. "What you mean 'shit'?"

"I mean, some of us don't got food to put on our tables neither," Art said.

"You look to me like you eat pretty good," Merlin said to Art, who was a large man. "You fat as a pig!"

"Look, Merlin," Eddie Gibbs said. Eddie played alto sax. He was the only musician, besides Merlin, who played in both bands. "We know that those sanitation workers in Memphis need our support. We're sympathetic. But some of us haven't worked in a long time. We've been living on borrowed money and looking forward to this gig to bail us out. Especially the new guys. Maybe we could reach a compromise. Donate only a half, say, or a third."

Merlin put his trumpet case down on a folding chair and opened it up. He had no intention of explaining about Benjamin. He could not have found the words. For Merlin, this concert, both the old music and the new, was a memorial to his slain son. He was in no mood to compromise or defend himself. Besides, Merlin had not developed a vocabulary for tenderness. *That* he expressed only with his trumpet. Anger translated quickly into words. Love and remorse were the territory of music only.

"Either you donate tonight's salary to the cause, or you ain't playing in Merlin Black's band," he said. "Now, is that clear or do I gotta say it again?"

"That sucks, Merlin," Art McLean said. "You just sore 'cause those demonstrators called you an Uncle Tom. We need the goddamn money!"

"Pack up your shit, Art, and vacate the premises," Merlin said, as he stuck the mouthpiece in his horn. "You out the band."

Tara decided that this wasn't her problem. She kissed Merlin on the cheek and walked out to the auditorium to hear the performance.

"What you gon' do without a bass player, Merlin?" Art shouted, furious.

"Lee can play electric bass as well as acoustic. Can't you, Lee?"

"Sure," said Lee Russell, a long-time member of Merlin's quintet. "But..."

"But what, Lee?" Merlin asked, silently blowing into his

mouthpiece and depressing the valves.

"Nothing, Merlin."

"Look, Merlin," Art said. "I'm sorry."

"Get the fuck outta here, Art. We don't need you. It don't take no goddamn genius to play bass."

Art McLean slammed his bass guitar back into its case.

"You bastard!" he said, as he stormed out.

"Anybody else want to complain?" Merlin asked. No one said anything. But it was clear that they were not happy. The air was thick with tension.

***

"Ladies and gentlemen," the announcer said. "We apologize for the delay. But we are ready, at last, for what promises to be an electric evening."

There were a few murmurs at the word "electric," but as the individual members of the quintet walked out on stage, just as their names were announced, they each were greeted with thunderous applause.

"On drums we have the always energetic Tommy Green. On bass, the versatile Lee Russell. On piano, the debonair Mr Sonny Potter. And on alto saxophone, the astonishing Eddie Gibbs." The musicians smiled tensely and greeted the capacity, standing-room-only audience.

"Before we bring him on stage," the announcer said. "I have been asked to announce that tonight's proceeds will be donated to the striking sanitation workers in Memphis, Tennessee, and to the good cause, down there, that's being led by the Reverend Martin Luther King.

"And now, the leader of the group..." The announcer dragged each word out slowly, deliberately milking the, already excited, audience. "The man of the hour. The one, the only Wizard of Jazz. Merlin Black!"

Merlin charged on stage, unsmiling. He turned his back to the audience. It was his trademark, his way of demanding respect, his way of saying: "I'm a proud, free black man, not a slave caricature, not a clown, who rolls his eyes and grins like Louis Armstrong." He nodded his head toward Tommy Green, the drummer and then launched into "My Foolish Heart," one of his most popular ballads. Only he was playing it at a breakneck tempo, twice the normal speed. Tommy Green took the cue and beat out a ferocious rhythm.

Merlin felt his adrenalin pumping like a freight train. He knew the other four musicians were angry at him. So what? he thought. Let them take their anger out on their instruments. He heard them pushing the volume, as well as the tempo, into overdrive.

The result was thrilling. The tender ballad, he had intended as a requiem for Benjamin was transformed into an anthem of anger. A song for 1968: a year that would soon bring political assassinations and nation-wide hysteria. A year which had just begun, but which had already seen massive demonstrations against the war in Vietnam, angry blacks burning down cities, and students, all over the country, capturing their universities and turning them into cauldrons of protest.

In the eye of that hurricane, one black man blew his heart and his soul into a trumpet. Merlin was so intense that, for a while, he lost all sense of who and where he was. He blew his own personal anger and hurt, mirroring his nation's agony, into a symphony of beauty and pain.

Whatever their motives might have been, the other members of the band kept pace with their leader. Each number came fast and furious. The audience loved it. When the musicians took a break, they were exhausted and drenched with sweat.

Tara met Merlin in his dressing room and kissed him on the cheek. "It's going great. You got them eating out of your hand."

"Yeah," he said, wiping the sweat from his forehead with a towel. "Hold on to your horses. Here comes the hard part."

***

During the intermission, the stage had been transformed. An electric organ replaced the piano. Everywhere else there were electronic devices and banks of speakers.

When Merlin came back on stage, he did something that he rarely did. He spoke to the audience.

"At this time, ladies and gentlemen, we'd like to welcome back Eddie Gibbs and Lee Russell." Eddie walked on with his sax, and Lee picked up an electric bass guitar. The applause was warm and enthusiastic.

"We'd like to introduce some new musicians now. Jesus Lopez on percussion." This time the applause was lukewarm and accompanied by some murmuring." On electric guitar — Al Bishop!" There was one loud and long "Boo!" coming from the back of the hall.

"On electric organ — Marcus LaPorta." Merlin could see the faces of the audience through the unreal glow, created by the stage lights. The auditorium was packed. Unreal people sat in neat rows on the ground level and in the balcony. Their dark yellow faces seemed placid, unnaturally calm.

He could distinguish both black and white, Negro and Caucasian, but more by their clothes and the features of their faces than by their color. All were bathed in a unnatural yellow, that made them seem oriental. Or maybe not so much oriental, as from a distant planet.

Merlin seldom looked at his audience. The critics called him arrogant, but he was, in truth, pathologically shy and easily intimidated. He was afraid. He was afraid of moments, such as this. Normally, he played smaller clubs. That was bad enough. But now, as he looked at this particular audience, New York's elite, he was hypnotized, paralyzed with fear.

Almost as in a dream, the quiet placidity of the audience was broken. He heard, before he saw, the angry, young man running down the left aisle toward him. Merlin felt a new stab of fear and his heart beat so fast, he had to gasp for breath. The protester was running toward him fast, but to Merlin it was happening in slow motion. Slower even than earlier, when he had rammed his car into the rear of the cab.

Finally, the demonstrator made it to the stage. His bent leg and his outstretched arm hit the edge, and he leapt up, deftly like an Olympic athlete clearing a hurdle. Merlin instinctively backed away from the microphone as the protester, a thin dashiki-clad man with a huge Afro-style haircut began to scream. Merlin could only watch and listen in silent fury.

"Mingus called…"

The protester was interrupted by catcalls, boos, and one piercing voice, crying out: "Louder! We can't hear you."

"Charles Mingus called jazz, 'Africa's Classical music'. We, of the African Awareness Committee, strongly protest this rape of our musical heritage."

"Yeah!" came voices from the back of the auditorium.

"Right on, brother!" rang out a bass voice from the balcony.

"Get the fuck off my stage," Merlin roared, holding his trumpet like a baseball bat.

"The white man raped our mothers and our grandmothers, producing bastards of no race. Now, this *Negro*…" The protester accented the word with all the venom he could muster, and there were several shouts of "Boo!" from different parts of the auditorium.

"This *Negro* wants to rape our classical music. Make it more like the white devil's effeminate and soulless rock 'n' roll. Can we allow him to do that?"

"No!" came the response from several directions.

"Get off my stage, nigger!" Merlin screamed and then swung the trumpet with all his might into the head of the protester, nicking him just above the right ear, which began to bleed immediately and profusely. Policemen rushed to the stage, grabbed the protester, and began to drag him off.

The audience turned into a mob. The few who supported Merlin stood and tried to shout down the protesters. Merlin brought the rest of the musicians on stage and began to play.

No one listened. The music was loud, but no one heard it. The audience simply shouted louder and drowned out the music. One of the protesters bashed his sign down on the head of a policeman. Several fights broke out. Another angry young man charged the stage and managed to unplug Al Bishop's electric guitar before the security people dragged him away.

As more fights broke out, the policemen began to spray mace on the combatants. The acrid smell reminded Merlin, once again, of Memphis and Benjamin. It grew worse until it dominated the entire auditorium.

"That's it!" Merlin said. "I'm outta here." Tara was waiting for him in the dressing room. As they came out of the building and turned down Seventh Avenue, the tears began to stream down his face. Tears stimulated by mace, but fueled by disappointment and rage. Tara noticed that Merlin was crying and put her right arm around his waist.

"I'm sorry, Merlin."

"This isn't what I meant," he sobbed. "This isn't what I fucking meant, at all."

Dr. Dover stopped for a second and glanced at his watch. "That's all the time we have today, but I'd like to pursue the topic of your mother with you next time. I think you need to confront her and decide just what it is that terrifies you so about her."

"Who says I'm terrified?" Merlin asked. His whole body tensed into a knot, as if to prove Dr. Dover's point.

"Are you?"

Merlin relaxed slightly and tried to think about the question. He didn't like to admit to being afraid of anything.

"Yes," he said after a long minute. He felt a single tear form under his right eye, which he immediately swept away. Merlin Black did not cry. "I guess maybe I am."

"Well, think about it, Merlin. Think about your mother and we'll talk about that next week."

"Doc, I need a new prescription."

"No, you don't Merlin." Russell Dover stood up and started to walk out of the office. "You've abused drugs most of your life. I won't be a party to…"

"Please, Doc," Merlin said. "Just some tranquilizers. I've got a really heavy gig coming up. I haven't played for five years. And I have to perform before a goddamn gadzillion people at the Hollywood fucking Bowl. I get so nervous just putting my trumpet to my mouth, I get the shakes. And I can't sleep."

Dr. Dover turned back around and looked at his patient. Merlin was wearing a black t-shirt, practically the same color as his skin. The shirt bore on it the face of a young Billie Holiday, with mouth parted, as if to sing, and a gardenia over her ear. He also wore baggy, purple gaucho pants with white polka dots.

"All right, Merlin. I'll write you up a prescription for a mild sedative. But you must not take more than one a day. Understood?"

"Solid, Doc!"

"I beg your pardon?"

"Uh… Thank you."

"Okay. See you next week."

Merlin found his Jaguar in the parking lot of the medical building and drove down Wilshire toward the ocean. He took the Santa Monica incline to the Pacific Coast Highway. He did not feel like going home to be alone. So, instead of turning right and going to his house in Malibu, he veered to the left and drove south.

First, he hit Venice, originally the fantasy of a wealthy Los Angeles businessman, who wanted to reproduce its namesake on the Adriatic. The fantasy had long since turned sour, and most of the canals had either been cemented over or had dried-up.

Venice had always been a magnet for the wild and disillusioned: sandal-clad beatniks in the 50's, day-glo hippies in the 60's, green-haired punks in the 80's. Merlin remembered the old days, especially the 50's, when he spent a lot of time here. Now although an uneasy mixture of yuppies, weight-lifters, the homeless, and the hopelessly spaced out, Venice still had its peculiar charms.

Merlin shifted over to Lincoln Boulevard and floated past Marina del Rey, solidly yuppie and relentlessly tidy and cheerful. He traveled past the airport, LAX, noisy and frightening, and El Segundo with its sweaty oilwells and dirty beaches. "If you lived in El Segundo," the sign read, "You'd be home by now."

He drove down a green hill, lined with pizza parlors and shopping malls, until he reached Manhattan Beach — sort of like Marina del Rey, only cheaper. It was the home of hip, young socialites and graduates of the college fraternity scene. And something else.

What was it? Oh, yeah, he thought, the McMartin Pre-School affair. Teachers accused of fucking children. Men and women teachers had been accused of abusing boys and girls, not old enough to be in the first grade. Just imagine, if it's true! Those white people are really perverted.

Finally, Merlin hit Hermosa Beach. He was trying hard to think about his mother like the Doc had ordered him to, but he couldn't stop thinking about Kimberly. He was really hooked on her. Hook, line, and sinker. Merlin was obsessed. He saw her only yesterday, but it felt like a longer time. He loved her and wondered if she would ever feel the same. He decided to call her later.

Merlin turned down the main drag and managed to find a parking place at the cul-de-sac, next to the pier, right in front of his destination — the Lighthouse. He got out of his car and looked inside the window. He had not been back here in years.

The Lighthouse had once been the chief jazz mecca of the entire west coast. Merlin had played here many times in the 50's. He had recorded live albums here. He had met his wife Cheryl for the very first time here. They were both basically New Yorkers, but they had met in this dusty, little dive in the sleepy L.A. suburb of Hermosa Beach, a long drive from Hollywood and light years away from 52nd Street in New York.

It seemed about the same to Merlin. It lay only a half block from the beach with its family style fishing pier. He smelled the same salty, slightly funky, sea air. The building had lost its tall lighthouse-like roof, but otherwise it hadn't changed. The dark panes of glass only barely concealed a small stage overlooking a few tables and a bar at the back.

It was so tiny. Probably not more than fifty or sixty people tops could be forced inside, if they were packed like sardines. But that's how it used to be. Jazz was performed in clubs like this, not at the Hollywood fucking Bowl. Not at Madison Square Garden or Yankee Stadium, and only on rare occasions at the Lincoln Center or at Carnegie Hall.

No, Merlin thought. All the great stuff — the music that Duke Ellington played and Count Bassie and Charlie Parker and Dizzy Gillespie and Thelonius Monk and Dexter Gordon, the Modern Jazz Quartet and dear, sweet, saint-like John Coltrane. It was all played in dirty, smokey, little dives like this. Mainly in New York: at the Savoy and at Minton's in Harlem, at the Three Deuces and the Onyx on 52nd Street, at the Vanguard and Cafe Bohemia in Greenwich Village. But also at the Plugged Nickel in Chicago, the Blackhawk in San Francisco, Peacock Alley in St. Louis, and at the Lighthouse in Hermosa Beach.

May 5, 1954

"Hey beautiful, where you been all my life?" Merlin was having difficulty standing up so he sat down, uninvited, at her table. He had not been able to keep his eyes off her. She had a round face with the deepest, most delicious dimples he had ever seen. She had light, smooth, cafe-au-lait skin and a supple, perfect body inside a sleek, black evening gown. But those eyes! Merlin felt he could just fall into those huge, brown, bottomless, meltingly-sweet eyes.

"I'm Merlin Black," he said.

"I know," Cheryl smiled. "We just heard you play. We came to the Lighthouse, especially to hear you."

Merlin looked over at her companion. She was very thin and nervous looking. It was difficult to make out her features through all that tobacco smoke, although he had no difficulty seeing Cheryl clearly. Feeling uneasy, he swayed a little in his chair and felt around in his coat pockets for a cigarette.

He was wearing a double-breasted, pin-striped suit with a thin, green tie, decorated with yellow diamonds, the kind of diamonds you see on playing cards. The diamonds had black dots in the middle of them, and the tie had been pulled, down and to the right, away from his top shirt button which was undone.

Merlin found a red and white pack of *Winston*'s in his inside coat pocket and pulled one out. He put the cigarette in his mouth backwards, pulled a box of matches out of his pants, and lit the match. He held the flickering match in front of his eyes for a moment. But it was no use. She refused to come into focus. At that point he sorta nodded out a little bit. At least, it felt as if he had gone to sleep or otherwise lost some time, when he heard her say:

"Merlin?"

Merlin zoomed the match over in the direction of the beautiful one, who was even more astonishingly beautiful when illuminated. How strange that he could see her so clearly, and the other one — not at all.

"What?" he finally managed to blurt out.

"You're about to light the filter."

"Oh!" Merlin shook the match out and dropped it in the

91

ashtray. That is, he attempted to drop it in the ashtray, but he missed. It fell right next to it, on the white tablecloth. In addition, he had not entirely succeeded in extinguishing the flame. He dabbed it hard with one quick jerk of his thumb, and it finally went out. Merlin turned the cigarette around and, with a little effort, managed to get the right end of it lit.

"What we need here is a drink." Merlin motioned for the waiter.

"Are you sure?" Cheryl asked. "Maybe you've had enough."

Merlin was still swaying back and forth in his chair.

"Enough?" he asked, scratching his left cheek vigorously. "I haven't had a drink all night."

The waiter came to the table, took their orders and left.

"You gonna wait around for the next set?" Merlin asked.

"If they don't throw us out."

"Naw. I won't let 'em throw you out. You're with me. You're with the band. Who are you, anyway?"

"I'm Cheryl James and this is my friend Bonnie Green."

"Hi, I'm Merlin Black." Merlin's cheek still itched badly, but he was afraid that if he scratched it any harder, it might start to bleed again.

The waiter brought the drinks. Merlin had ordered a martini, Cheryl a Scotch and soda, Bonnie a Manhattan.

Merlin jerked his glass high in the air, spilling some of the clear liquid onto the table.

"Well, here's to you, Cheryl James and…"

"Bonnie Green," Bonnie reminded him.

"Right! I knew that. Here's to you both!"

Merlin downed his drink in one gulp.

"Waiter!"

"Yes, Mr Black?" the waiter said.

"Another round for Cheryl James and Whazzer-face. And me too. Another martini."

"Yes, sir. Very good."

"And waiter?" Merlin extinguished his cigarette which he had smoked all the way down to the filter.

"Yes, sir?"

"Put it on my tab."

The waiter turned to leave.

"And, waiter?"

"Yes, Mr Black?"

"Forget the fucking vermouth, would ya?"

"Yes, sir."

"How long have you lived in Hermosa Beach, Cheryl James?"

"But I don't live here, Merlin."

"Well then, where do you live?"

"In Manhattan. On 32nd Street."

"No, kidding! So do I. Well, not on 32nd Street. But in Manhattan."

"I know."

"You do?"

"Yes."

"How come?"

"You're famous."

The waiter brought the second round of drinks. Neither Cheryl nor Bonnie had finished the first. "You're on again in ten minutes, Mr Black."

"Yeah? Who told *you*?"

"Mr Kelly, the owner. He just told me to remind you."

"Yeah? Well, you tell him for me to fuck-off. Would you do that?"

"Yes, sir." The waiter deposited the drinks and left.

Merlin again socked back his drink in a single swallow.

"So you've heard of me, have you?"

"Yes," Cheryl said. "I have a huge stack of your records. Maybe not everything you ever recorded, but almost."

"Really? Which is your favorite?"

"Well, I love the new one, 'Stranger in Paradise'." Cheryl took another sip of her drink. She leaned back in her chair and smiled. Her dimples deepened. Merlin's heart sank. He could not remember ever having found a woman so beautiful before.

"But I guess my all-time favorite is 'But Not For Me'," she said. "The one you did with Charlie Parker."

"Waiter!"

"Yes, Merlin?"

Merlin lit another cigarette and leaned back in his chair, as Cheryl had just done. He tried to remain calm and not to stare holes into her. Slowly his attention turned to the waiter, and he realized that he had just been addressed by the first name.

"Oh, it's 'Merlin' now, is it? It was 'Mr Black' earlier. Never

93

mind. Bring me another drink."

"Mr Kelly told me not to serve you another drink before you went on stage."

"Oh, he did, did he? Did you tell him to fuck-off, like I told you to?"

"Yes, sir."

"Well, what did he say?"

"That's when he told me not to serve you any more alcohol and to remind you that the last set will begin shortly."

Merlin puffed out smoke and looked back at the two women. They had still not finished their first drink nor begun their second.

"Can I see you after the set is over."

"Sure," Cheryl said. Her companion looked uncomfortable and then whispered something in her ear. Cheryl whispered something back and then said: "Yeah, we'll wait."

When Merlin returned to the stage, he stuck the mute in his trumpet. He stepped up to the mike.

"I'd like to play 'But Not For Me' for Miss Cheryl James and her friend. Course it ain't true what it says in the lyrics. 'Cause someone *is* 'writing songs of love' for you. And that would be me."

He stepped back from the mike and blew through his horn. The sound came out soft and lovely with just a touch of melancholy. The room was only about half filled. It was Thursday night, not one of the club's busy weekend nights. Still cigarette smoke surrounded the room like a cloud.

Merlin was not at the peak of his popularity. Far from it. The heady days with Charlie Parker were over, and Merlin had been in a slump. Jobs were few and far between in Manhattan. The big bands had died. No one was listening to jazz. It was all 'How Much Is That Doggie in the Window'? and similar pop with safe, white, squeaky clean singers like Eddie Fisher, Patti Page, and Tennessee Ernie Ford.

Merlin had become despondent and bitter. He had begun to use heroin. It seemed like everyone did now. Charlie Parker had made it fashionable. At first, Merlin only snorted it. After that, he did a little skin popping. But then one day he shot up. And the next day. And the next.

Everybody in his band used: John Coltrane — his tenor saxophone man, the drummer, the piano player, the bass player. Peter Pollard, his soft-spoken arranger, Merlin's only white friend at the moment, was shooting up like the rest of them.

Merlin didn't have much need for an arranger at this point in his career. But Peter traveled with the band. He could play almost any instrument and sat in, if one of the regular band members was too stoned to play. Also, he could score more easily than the rest — at least in Los Angeles — because, he *was* white.

Merlin finished his solo and walked off the stage. Peter Pollard was in the back room.

"Peter, I need a fix."

Peter was very thin. He looked a bit like a hayseed, but he was very hip. He was married to a black woman, and spent most of his life with black people.

"Not cool. Merlin. Not here. Not a good time."

"I need a fucking fix." Merlin ripped off his coat and rolled up his sleeve. He pulled off the tie, the one with all those yellow diamonds on it and tied it around his upper left arm.

"What if I told you I don't have any shit, Merlin? That I'm not holding?"

"I'd call you a goddamn liar."

"At least, go in the john for god's sake! I'll cook up a shot for you."

Merlin opened the door to the bathroom, walked in one of the stalls, and sat down. His mind wandered off in several different directions, but mainly he was thinking about Cheryl James. He hadn't cared about a woman in years. He still saw Harriet occasionally when he went home to Memphis. But that wasn't often.

He saw his two sons, as well, Benjamin and Eugene. He loved them, especially Benjamin, and had sent them as much money as he could. But he hadn't cared about Harriet in years. Not really. She had never forgiven him for not marrying her.

There had been a white woman in France, when he had gone there a few years earlier. But that was only a summer romance. It hadn't amounted to much. Just mainly the novelty of fucking a white chick.

So it was odd, he thought. Very odd, indeed, that he was so besotted with Cheryl James immediately and instantaneously. Love at first sight. Had anyone suggested such a thing to him earlier in the day, he would have laughed in their face.

Merlin leaned back on the toilet seat, his head against the wall, and closed his eyes. The tie was still wound around his arm. He almost nodded off again. He was going to have to take something to wake up. He had some bennies somewhere in his dressing room.

Suddenly, he became very aware of Trane's solo. Dear, sweet, gentle John Coltrane, making very ungentle sounds. Making wonderful ripples of music. The massive tenor spluttered, soared, and plummeted in giant swoops of sound — hard, loud, and funky. The saxophone's a more versatile horn than the trumpet, he thought.

My poor, little trumpet is actually a very limited instrument, used mainly for marches. Triumphal Fucking March from *Aida*. His fingers depressed imaginary valves. Ta TAAAH! Ta Ta Ta TAAAH, Ta-Ta-Ta, TAAAAH TAAH TAAH. Only, I stick my Harmon Mute into it and make it sing. Like Caruso at the fucking Met. I make it sing songs of love and pain.

The people hear it and cry tears of pleasure. They think they know where my pain comes from. But, they don't know shit. Nobody. Nobody knows. "Nobody knows de trouble I seen."

By the time Peter brought the syringe into the bathroom, Merlin was laughing loudly and singing:

"Nobody kno-o-o-ows but Jesus."

"Merlin," Peter whispered. "They can hear you out there."

"Oh!" Merlin said, awakening from his reverie. "I'm sorry, Peter. You got the shit?"

Peter held out a syringe.

"You want me to do the honors?"

"Would you?"

"Give me a vein."

Merlin tightened the tie and tensed his arm. There were track marks from previous injections all the way from the arm pit to the fingers. Peter found a vein and stuck the needle in.

"Next time you're gonna have to use your leg, Merlin. Not much room left."

Merlin closed his eyes. He felt the needle go in his arm and the juice flow through his vein. God! Jesus! he thought, as he anticipated and quickly consummated the wild rush of excitement, the fast flow of energy and warmth into every pore. God, that's good. Like sex. Like coming hard. Only all over my body.

"Thanks, Peter. I owe you one."

***

Later, after the set was over, and the other woman, Bonnie Green, Whazzer-face, had left in her Ford and gone home to Watts, Merlin gave Cheryl his car keys. He said he was too wired to drive. And he was, because he had swallowed several uppers on his last trip to the dressing room. But he didn't tell her that part.

So Cheryl got behind the wheel of his car, a new, white Oldsmobile. He liked to be in control of white things. Merlin had sold his last car, a red Corvette, for smack money. But then he had landed a new record contract and had been able to afford a down payment on the Olds. At Merlin's suggestion, Cheryl drove to the Santa Monica Pier.

"You played both of my favorite numbers," Cheryl smiled up at Merlin, through her cloud of pink cotton candy. The Santa Monica Pier was a year-round carnival, a continual country fair and more. There was a giant carousel with about fifty, smiling, wooden horses tinkling up and down, in front of garish red and green lights, and behind loud, calliope music.

There were Guess-Your-Weight Booths and Win-A-Teddy-Bear Booths, Body Builders, and a Tattooed Fat Lady. There were also restuarants and shops and shady looking characters selling dope and pornography.

"Yeah," Merlin said, almost smiling, wanting to smile, but looking as if the smile might crack his face. "I hope you liked 'Stranger In Paradise'."

"I did. Thank you."

Since Cheryl had come to the Lighthouse specifically to meet Merlin, she was not disappointed. Even though he acted erratic, it only added to his mystique. His eyes, when she could see them, were deep and piercing. But mainly he wore sunglasses, even though it was night-time.

He was a small man, but Cheryl, who was only five-foot-four herself didn't mind that. He was thin, almost skinny. His face was round, the skin color dark and shiny.

"This place reminds me of the State Fair when I was a kid," he said.

"Yeah, me too. Where you from?"

"Memphis." Merlin was mellow from the heroin, but wired from the bennies. He wondered if she knew he was high. He itched all over and worried that he was sweating too much.

"Where you from?"

"St. Louis."

"Yeah?" Merlin said, peering down at her, over his sunglasses which had slipped way down on his nose. "So what is it that you do, that takes you from St. Louis to New York to Hermosa Beach?"

"I'm a dancer with the American Ballet Theater. What they call a 'featured dancer'. They pride themselves on being very liberal and advanced, but apparently not quite advanced enough yet to have a Negro 'principal dancer'."

"What's the difference?"

"Well, 'featured dancers' get to do secondary roles in major full-length ballets, or, sometimes, major roles in short ones." Cheryl deposited most of her cotton candy, having only eaten a few bites into a trash can, as they passed by it.

"Ever been to a ballet?" she asked.

"No," Merlin said. "But I'll come see *you* anytime. When do you dance next in New York?"

They stopped at a booth, and Merlin pitched three plastic rings toward a stick in an unsuccessful attempt to win Cheryl a teddy bear.

"Next month, as a matter of fact. We're doing *Swan Lake* at the Metropolitan Opera House. But don't blink, or you'll miss me. I mean, they make a big deal out of hiring a black person for the company, and then they do the best they can to hide me."

"Here," Merlin said, taking off his dark glasses and handing them to Cheryl. "Maybe I'll do better without these."

He handed the man fifty cents for three more plastic rings and squinted at the wooden stick around which he must toss at least two of the rings, or there would be no teddy bear. Like Cheryl's friend Whazzer-face, the wooden stick refused to come into focus. In fact, the harder Merlin stared at it the more blurred it became.

"I mean, the role of the black swan would be a natural,"Cheryl continued. "Don't ya think?"

Merlin carefully took aim and tossed the first ring. With a

shudder, it hit the target and encircled the stick successfully. Merlin felt elated at this accomplishment.

"What?" he said. "I'm sorry. What did you say?"

"They ought to let me dance the role of Odile, the black swan, in *Swan Lake* or maybe the chosen one in *The Rite of Spring*."

Merlin threw the second ring and missed.

"*The Rite of Spring*," he said. "Is that the one by Stravinsky?"

"Yes," Cheryl said, folding Merlin's glasses and putting them in her small, red handbag. "Do you know it?"

"Yes. The music. I love it. Actually, Igor and I are very good friends. He lives in Santa Monica, you know?" Merlin again loosened his tie, the same one he had used to raise a shooting vein in his arm, earlier in the evening.

"Really?"

"Yeah. Not more than five miles from here."

"No. I mean, you and Igor Stravinsky are good friends?"

Merlin held the third and last ring poised in the air and squinted down at Cheryl.

"You would believe me if I told you that Igor was my main man?"

"Sure, Merlin. I'd believe anything you say."

Merlin tossed the yellow, plastic ring and missed.

"Shit!"

"Mr Black!" Cheryl said. "You forget you're with a lady."

Merlin looked at Cheryl, the enormous, brown eyes and those dimples spread all over her cheeks by a sly smile.

"No," he said. "I haven't forgotten. Hey, you!" Merlin called to the barker, a tall white man wearing suspenders, a bow tie, and a straw hat.

"Yes, sir? Want to try again? Just fifty cents for three tosses."

"Would you just sell me one of those teddy bears?"

"Sell you a teddy bear?" The barker looked confused.

"Merlin," Cheryl said. "I don't need a teddy bear. Really!"

"How much?" Merlin persisted.

"Twenty-five dollars."

"Twenty-five dollars! You've got to be joking!"

"Take it or leave it," the barker said.

"All right. I'll take it." Merlin pulled some loose bills out of his pants pocket.

"You want the white bear or the brown bear?"

"The brown one," Merlin muttered. "I don't want no honky bears."

Merlin took the bear and presented it to Cheryl. "Here's your bear, Miss Cheryl James. I think you ought to call him Mr Ralph Bunche Bear or Mr Joe Louis Bear."

Cheryl took the bear and flashed her irresistible smile once again. "Not Mr Merlin Black Bear?"

"Definitely not," Merlin said. "I wouldn't wish that name on any defenseless teddy bear."

"Where'd you get it?"

"Where'd I get what?"

"Your name. 'Merlin'?"

"My mother was hung-up on King Arthur stories."

"Oh," Cheryl said, hugging her bear. "So, do you know Igor Stravinsky or not?"

"No, I really don't. But I think we ought to go over there and introduce ourselves."

"Oh, really? I'm sure Igor Stravinsky would just welcome two strange Negroes off the street right into his house. Especially this late at night. More likely, he'd call the cops."

"You want a hot dog?"

"I'm supposed to keep trim. I'm a dancer. Remember?"

Merlin looked up and down her perfect body. "You're plenty trim, Cheryl."

"That's the first time you called me by my first name alone."

"It is?"

"Yes, you usually say 'Cheryl James' or 'Miss Cheryl James'. Does that mean we're going to be friends?"

Merlin watched her, still hugging the teddy bear and batting her long eyelashes, and his heart sank into his feet.

"Only if you have a hot dog with me."

"Well, okay," she said. "It's a deal."

They walked to the hot dog stand, near the end of the pier. It was a bright, clear spring night. The moon was almost full and the stars sparkled and glowed. Merlin had the man put everything on his hot dog: mustard, ketchup, pickle relish, onions, the works. Cheryl had only mustard on hers.

They turned to walk back toward the front end of the pier. The beach was illuminated by the moon and stars. It was lit up, and eerie, glowing white and yellow against the dark landscape of the Santa Monica Mountains to the north and the city straight ahead.

A white man walked by them, headed in the opposite direction. His elbow lightly brushed up against Merlin's arm, just as Merlin was about to take the first bite of his hot dog.

"They let these goddamn niggers go everywhere now," the white man muttered.

"What did you say?" Merlin turned around to look at the back of the man walking away from him. The man stopped and turned around.

"Are you talking to me?" He was a fat, balding man in a large, double-breasted suit. He looked like a menacing Lou Costello.

"Yes, I'm talking to you. Who else?"

"Merlin," Cheryl said. "Don't provoke him."

"Where I come from," the man said. "Colored people address their betters as 'sir'."

"Where I come from we call scum like you 'poor white trash'."

With that, Merlin hurled his hot dog toward the man and hit him in the chest. The mustard and ketchup stained his shirt and suit, as the bun and contents slid off.

"Come on, nigger. Come on!" The man threw off his coat and began to remove his tie.

"Merlin, please don't do this," Cheryl said.

Merlin did not bother to take off his coat. He pushed the white man in the chest with his palms. He then grabbed his tie, which the white man had not yet removed. Merlin yanked the thin end of the tie until the knot was at the man's throat and continued tightening the tie until the man began to choke.

The man grabbed Merlin's neck with both hands. He choked Merlin until Merlin was gasping and then shoved his knee hard into Merlin's groin. Merlin recoiled in pain, loosening his grip on the man's tie. The white man then slugged Merlin in the jaw. Merlin felt the blow, and he wanted to fight back.

The pain in his crotch and the heroin in his body, however, made him slow to react. He saw the second blow coming. The man hit him in the stomach, and Merlin bowled over in pain. Then the man's knee caught Merlin under the chin. He fell on

101

his side hard against the wooden boardwalk.

"Had enough, nigger?"

"Fuck you, honky!" Merlin was holding his stomach and rocking in pain.

"What did you say, nigger?"

"Fuck you," Merlin whispered. He could not summon enough air to shout. Most of the nearby people hurried away from the fight, but three white men had come closer. They were cheering the demented Lou Costello look-alike.

"I didn't hear you, nigger. What did you say?"

"Fuck you, honky," Merlin hissed at a clearly audible level.

"That's what I thought you said." The man proceeded to kick Merlin in the side and in the face to the cheers and applause of the three onlookers. After about five kicks, and, as the blood began to gush from the side of Merlin's face, Cheryl intervened. She ran up to the man and began to beat him on the chest.

"Stop it! Stop it! Leave him alone!"

Finally the man left, but not until after he spat on the seemingly unconscious Merlin. The three onlookers cheered him again and walked off with him, patting him on the back.

"Merlin?" Cheryl knelt down by her fallen date. She was terrified. She had first been afraid for Merlin's life, and now she was still afraid that he was severely injured.

"Yeah?" Merlin opened his bloodied and swollen eyes.

"Are you okay?"

"I've had better days." He smiled. It was the first time she had seen him smile broadly. She laughed, and then they both laughed.

"Do you want to go to the hospital?"

"Naw, they will kill me *there* for sure."

Merlin began to stand up, slowly and methodically. He felt around his right eye.

"Did he knock off my shades?"

"No," Cheryl said. "You gave them to me when you were throwing the rings. Remember?"

"Oh, yeah."

"You want them?"

"Yeah," Merlin said, straightening out his coat and dusting off his pants. "Don't forget Joe Louis Bear. Where was he when I needed him?"

102

Merlin limped off toward the parking lot, holding his side. Cheryl retrieved the bear and her abandoned purse. She helped Merlin to the white Olds, and then drove him to his hotel room in Hollywood.

***

The room was set up on the hill overlooking Sunset Boulevard and boasted an impressive view of the night lights of Los Angeles. Merlin found a bottle of gin and poured a drink for both of them. He threw his coat and tie on the bed and unbuttoned the top button of his shirt.

Cheryl went to the bathroom to get a wash cloth to wipe the blood off his face, and Merlin threw himself down into a chair, with large, green cushions. The cool cloth felt good on his face. He allowed himself to relax while she softly cleaned his bruises. As she was bending over him, he smelled a sweet odor from her soft, shapely breasts, gently wiggling to the rhythm of her movements. He wanted to bend closer and kiss the delicious flesh just in front of his eyes. But he didn't.

"How does my lip look?" he asked instead. "Motherfucker hurt my lip, I won't be able to play."

Cheryl pulled back and inspected his mouth.

"There is a little cut right here." She bent down and kissed him softly on the cut part of his lip. "Does that hurt?"

Merlin looked up at her, feeling himself falling in love deeper and harder. This wasn't real. His anger and his pain were suddenly gone. And he was lost in the mystery of love. Or lust or whatever it was. Merlin didn't know. He only knew that he had never felt this way before. Certainly not with Harriet.

No, the feeling was absolutely new, yet somehow familiar. It was unsought, but it changed everything. Forever. A tear formed in his right eye and slowly ran down his cheek. He made no effort to wipe it away.

"Did I hurt you?"

"Yes," Merlin said. "But not in the way you mean."

"In what way then?"

"When I look in your face, it hurts." Merlin meant it. His feelings for Cheryl hurt much more deeply than the wounds his body had received in the fight. She hurt him in some primordial way — like birth or death.

Cheryl stood upright. "I think I'm insulted."

Merlin put his arms around her waist. He drew her to him and placed his head on her stomach.

"Don't be. I love you."

"Yeah," Cheryl said, trying to keep the tone of the conversation light. "But will you respect me in the morning?"

Merlin pulled away from her slightly, and looked up at her face, shining with a beauty that seemed to increase each time he saw it.

"No, Cheryl. I mean it."

She looked down at his face. His right eye was bruised and swollen. There was a cut on his lip and a bloodied scab on his ear. The tears were flowing freely from both eyes now.

"I think you *do* mean it," she said. She was genuinely surprised. She felt that she had known Merlin for a long time. She had a crush on the pensive, shy man who blew sad and romantic songs through his horn. She had cried often listening to his music. It touched the deepest part of her.

She had gone after him, not really believing that she would get him. She was only a fan pursuing a star, a public personality. A man famous to all American Negroes as a symbol of uncompromising dignity. A man who had refused to play Negro stereotypes. He never rolled his eyes or told jokes or acted dumb. He never pandered to the tastes or the expectations of a white audience.

He was a strong black prince, a stern and serious minded genius who played, not dance music, but searing melodies. Deeply romantic and sad music — like her beloved Tchaikovsky. It had that same quality. It made her shiver and somehow it made her happy too, to know that she was not alone in feeling sad or in wanting more.

She would have been happy with an autograph.

Cheryl began to unbutton the other buttons on his shirt and, when they were undone, she pulled the garment off his back. She was shocked by the sight of the needle marks all over his arms.

"My God," she said. "What's wrong with you?"

"I'm a diabetic," Merlin lied, looking down at the floor. He was embarrassed and could not look her in the face.

"Oh," Cheryl said. "Take that undershirt off. Let's see if that

104

fool really hurt you."

"Oh, shit! I was hoping you were tryin' to undress me, because you wanted my body."

"Take off that undershirt! And I mean right now." Cheryl flashed her wry smile at him. The truth was she really did want him and would sleep with him if he made a move.

With some difficulty, Merlin pulled off his undershirt. Cheryl knelt down to take a look. His whole side, from the arm pit to the hip, was livid. She touched it gently, gingerly.

"Does that hurt?"

"Shit!" Merlin jumped. "No. It feels good. Do it again."

"I think you should go to the emergency room."

"Ain't going to no emergency room." Merlin got up and poured himself another drink from the gin bottle.

"Cheryl, will you stay with me tonight?"

"Yes, Merlin." Cheryl stood up and walked over to him.

"I can't," he said, putting his glass down on the table. Then he turned around and stared at her. "I can't..."

"You can't what, Merlin?" Cheryl drew closer to him.

"I can't... You know... have sex."

"I know, Merlin. You're all beat up. It would hurt you."

"No. It's more than that."

"Well, what?" Cheryl drew close to him and gently put her arms around his waist.

"What, Merlin?"

"I..." Merlin put his arms around *her* waist and drew her even closer. "I'm sick," he whispered.

"You have syphilis? Gonorrhea? Something like that?"

"No. No. Nothing like that."

"Well, what?"

"I can't tell you."

"Is it your diabetes?"

"Sort-of."

"Those aren't insulin shots. Are they, Merlin?"

"No, Cheryl. They're something else."

"I thought so."

"I know what I have to do now to get well." He smelled the sweetness of her hair. The top of her head came right to the level of his nose. "Before... before, I didn't want to do it. But now... now, I do."

"Kimberly?"

"Merlin, is that you?" Kimberly had just gotten out of the shower. She was getting ready for a date. She stood, clutching a towel to her dripping body.

"Yes. Hi'ya doin'?"

"Where are you, Merlin? You sound like you're at the end of a tunnel?"

"I'm on a public phone." Merlin called Kimberly from an outside phone at the end of the cul-de-sac in Hermosa Beach. In front of him, he viewed the cemented pathway that ran over the beach, from the sidewalk to the pier.

He heard the waves lapping loudly on the shore, and a cacophony of other sounds as well. The sea gulls shouted out their indignant protests. Bikini-clad roller skaters, drinking *Evian* and eating corn-dogs, screamed to each other as they sailed past him. Punk looking surfers carried large, shrieking ghettoblasters, and motorcycles roared-up and back-fired in all directions.

Merlin stuck a finger in his left ear to minimize the noise.

"I'm in Hermosa Beach."

"Where?"

"Hermosa Beach. Do you know where that is?"

"Of course. I'm a native. Remember?"

"Come on down."

"What? I can't hear you." Kimberly adjusted the towel again, which she kept bunching together under her arms, and which kept coming loose.

"I said, come on down." Merlin moved closer into the little shell that surrounded, barely, the pay phone, in hopes that the acoustics would improve.

"Merlin, I can't. I have a date."

"Break it."

"Merlin!"

"All right. All right. How about tomorrow? Can we work on the book?"

"I guess so. Will you be at home?"

"No. I'll be here."

Kimberly found herself getting more and more pulled into

Merlin's world. She had worked on the book for three weeks, and it was the most exciting thing she had ever done. Her own life seemed automatic and colorless compared to his. His was a glamorous, if somewhat depraved, lifestyle. She loved his music, and she was also attracted to him as a person. In spite of herself, she was falling in love with him.

She knew that she would really rather go meet Merlin in Hermosa Beach than to go on this nowhere date. She was seeing a man, Harvey Wilson, whom she had met at her A.A. meeting. He wasn't much fun, and Kimberly was truly tempted to break the date. But she would not do it. It was a matter of principle. And besides she was a little afraid of Merlin and the emotions he aroused in her.

"You'll be where?"

"Hermosa Beach. Kimberly, I thought I explained that. Are you drunk or something?"

"No, Merlin. I don't drink. And I know 'Hermosa Beach'. But can you be a little more specific? *Where* in Hermosa Beach?"

Merlin looked over behind the Lighthouse and saw the name of a motel.

"At the Sea Sprite Motel."

"Okay. Noon?" Kimberly finally just gave up on her towel and let it fall to the floor.

"Noon's fine."

"Why Hermosa Beach?"

"Well, you told me to stir up some memories, didn't you?"

"Yes."

"Well, that's what I'm doing. Stirring up some memories."

Merlin and Cheryl were married in January. In New York. Merlin had never been happier. He was madly in love with his new bride. They honeymooned in Jamaica in a cottage near Montego Bay. They lay on the picture-perfect beach and gazed out at the azure waters. The days were warm and lazy. The nights were cool and beautiful. They walked barefoot on the beach and embraced under an enormous moon. They ate mangoes, tangerines, ackee, goat curry, and jerk chicken. They danced at the local clubs.

One club in particular, not the usual tourist trap, but a place where Jamaicans went. It was tiny. It was open air, letting in all the smells and humidity and the moonlight, dripping through like a rich cream. A few tables hugged the small dance floor, where they sipped fruity drinks from coconut shells: rum punch, Planter's punch, zombies. But not too much. Not enough to spoil the greater high Merlin got from staring into Cheryl's face.

He looked in her eyes. They sparkled. They smiled. He was always drawn to her eyes. That's where the emotion was. She had so many different looks. She was so many different women. But it began in the eyes, which transformed the rest of her, even the size and shape of her body.

She was so round and fleshy in bed when they made love, listening only to the sound of wind through the palm trees. So thin in the morning, while he watched her dress. She was self-conscious about that. As if he were looking at her imperfections, invading her privacy. But Merlin saw no imperfection. He delighted in her beauty in all its infinite variety. As now, on the tiny dance floor.

She was wearing a tight, cotton dress that showed off all her delicious contours. He danced, thinking only of her. Merlin seldom danced. Odd, in a way, for a man who played music all his life. But now dancing was an excuse for gazing without apology. For staring at the beauty of Cheryl, which never faded, never waned. It changed. But it only grew deeper, more complex.

He feared only that he would drown in her love. Would not be able to find his way back. Back to what? What had he done

108

before he met Cheryl?

Merlin fell in love too with the scenery — with Jamaica. He'd never seen a place so green. All around them were trees, plants and shrubs. The island was populated mainly with black people. Strong, proud, black people. They spoke with an accent that was English and yet African, as well.

"Yeh, mon. We happy to ave de famous Merlin Black wid us inna Jah-MAY-kah. How lang yuh ah stay? T'ree weeks? Dats all, mon? Well, any t'ing you need. No problem. Any t'ing, a'tall."

And everywhere they heard music. Wonderful music that beat with the rhythm of Africa, laced with the charm of Latin America. Calypso, ska, steal drums, guitars, bongos.

And everywhere too there was Cheryl. Shopping in Mo' Bay. On the beach, gorgeous in her bathing suit. Warm in his bed. He was hypnotized by her face, and he memorized every inch of her body. Her flesh was like no other. He thrilled to her touch. He never tired of her embrace. He had kicked his drug habit. Drank liquor, only moderately. He no longer needed narcotics. He was intoxicated with his wife. He never believed it could be this good.

Back in the states, Merlin began to put some Caribbean influences into his music. Nothing obvious. Nothing derivative. But he did not stop there. He continued to expand. He listened to everything he could get his hands on. His music was all a giant stew, into which Merlin kept adding ingredients: the sound of the mariachi bands of Mexico, mambo, bossa nova, Calypso, cancion mexicana, the marimba dance, conga. He even listened to European classical music: Mozart, Bach, avant-garde, atonal, electronic.

But no matter what he added, the result was always Merlin Black. It was always his own, and unique.

He obtained a powerful new agent, named Barry Franklin, who got him a contract with RCA.

Merlin collaborated with Peter Pollard for a series of big band, or rather, orchestral records. The first was called *Memories of Jamaica*. Then he did a jazz interpretation of Verdi's *Aida*. And finally a work simply called *Africa*. He journeyed to Africa to study the indigenous folk music. He went to the Cameroons and Kenya. He went to Egypt and Ethiopia. And Cheryl went with him. She gave up her dancing to be with him.

Merlin's albums sold well. There was a new interest in jazz in the late 50's and 60's. The beatniks in San Francisco and Greenwich Village, and the weekend beatniks all across America, were addicted to jazz. The Ivy League fraternity boys thrived on jazz. They all bought Merlin's records. The quintet recordings sold in the hundreds of thousands. The orchestral records sold even better.

Merlin rented a luxury apartment, overlooking Central Park, on the upper east side at 79th Street. He and Cheryl worked hard to fix it up really nice. Cheryl wanted to have children. Merlin didn't. He pointed out that he already had two sons. Now that he was married he wanted to do more for them. He sent larger checks home to Harriet, but he wanted to spend more time with them, as well.

Cheryl talked about resuming her career. Merlin did not encourage her, but neither did he stop her.

So, Cheryl began to get up early in the morning for lessons. Merlin's life was at night. He slept in the daytime. They saw less and less of each other. Cheryl no longer accompanied Merlin when he went out on tours.

It was inevitable that Merlin would attract other women. He was handsome. He was an icon. His picture was everywhere: on magazine covers, in the newspaper, on album covers, and billboards. Merlin resisted temptation. Most of the time. Until he met Tara Marlowe.

It wasn't until after Merlin had cheated on Cheryl, that he became jealous. If he could do it, so could she. He was suspicious of any man who paid her the slightest attention.

He stopped believing her. He was certain that she was lying, when she said that she was not sleeping with anyone else. He slapped her. After the first time, he felt terrible. He began to drink more. The second time he hit her was easier. The bitch deserves it, he thought. Not only is she fucking around, but she lies about it.

Merlin was asked to play at a jazz concert at Antibes in the south of France, partly because he knew that Tara would be at the nearby Cannes Film Festival. He arranged several other gigs in Europe, where he was very popular. One in Berlin and another at the Odeon at the foot of the Acropolis in Athens. He asked Cheryl to come with him. To his considerable surprise, she accepted.

The evening of the performance at Antibes, Merlin did not come back to their hotel room. He spent the night with Tara.

"Where have you been?" Cheryl asked the next morning. She wore a green negligée over her bathing suit.

The room was filled with sunlight which bounced off the pastel pink of the bedspread and the buttery gold of the walls.

"I had to listen to the tapes of the concert, Cheryl. The engineers insisted. They have to touch them up with over-dubs." Cheryl didn't believe him. She knew him too well.

Cheryl loved Merlin, but she was fed up. He was drinking heavily now. She wouldn't be surprised if he were using drugs, as well. She knew he was seeing other women, or, at least, another woman. She had no proof, didn't know who it was, or care. But she knew.

She understood, to a degree, the pressures on Merlin. That he lived in a world of night clubs, where everyone drank or took drugs. Where men and women were loose and horny and on the lookout for a mate, temporary or permanent.

But she would not, could not, just stand by and watch Merlin fall back down into that hole where she had first found him. She couldn't reason with him. God knows, she had tried. He was difficult. And fame and fortune had given him an excuse to be arrogant.

"Do you expect me to believe that?"

"I need a drink, Cheryl. Would you fix me something?"

"No."

"I told you RCA's gonna release last night's concert as a live recording. I told you that, didn't I?"

Cheryl went over to the dresser. She poured a tall glass full of gin. She walked back to the bed where her husband lay and poured the entire contents on his unsuspecting face. Then she walked out of the hotel room into the bright, Mediterranean sunlight.

***

Merlin strolled through the ancient streets of Athens. Tara was waiting for him in one of the hotels of the Plaka, near Syntagma Square. He walked past the small reception room to the tiny elevator. It jerked and creaked and moved so slowly,

Merlin thought he would never get to the third floor.

Tara was waiting for him with champagne and ouzo.

He embraced her and pulled down the straps of her black, silky nightgown. He kissed her mouth, her neck, between her breasts. He caressed and licked each nipple, slowly and tenderly. He fell to his knees and pulled her sex to his face, smelling the sweet, strong odor of her, and exploring her vulva with his tongue.

***

Cheryl pretended to be asleep when Merlin returned at dawn. She listened to him undress. She knew he was drunk by the awkwardness of his movements, stumbling in the early morning light. And when he lay down beside her, she smelled not only the liquor, but the other woman, as well. Smelled the infidelity.

One person is not interchangeable for another, she thought. You can't just trade an old model in, for a newer one, as if people were automobiles. And what have I done to make myself outmoded? Why have I lost him? I gave up my career only to be with him, and went back to it, only because I suspected he had grown bored with me.

I wanted to give him children, but he wouldn't let me. I haven't grown fat, or old, or ugly. Maybe this is just a stage. A fling. Maybe he'll get over it and come back to me.

June 29, 1990

After talking to Kimberly, Merlin walked back up Pier Avenue until he found a drug store. He had the prescription that Dr. Dover had given him and while he was waiting, he bought a bottle of vodka. Then he went back to his car and drove to the Sea Sprite Motel.

Although the room was divided into three levels, it appeared small and cramped. Compared to his house in Malibu, the ceilings seemed especially low.

The bed and TV covered most of the lowest level. The next level, two steps up from the bedroom, contained a refrigerator and a table, which stood by the only window. Two more steps led to a tiny alcove with a closet on one side and the entrance to the bathroom on the other.

Merlin took a nap, and, when he woke up, he fixed himself a drink. He washed down two of the tranquilizers with straight vodka and got ready to go to the Lighthouse.

It was only 8:15, and the Lighthouse didn't open until nine. Merlin walked up the street until he spotted a bar called Pier 66.

He looked inside. The place was packed. Hundreds of young people, mainly white, danced to a pulsing rock and roll band. There was a swirling, ever blinking and changing light show of the kind that was popular in the discos of the 1970's.

Merlin walked in and ordered a drink, vodka with a twist. The tranquilizers kicked in, and Merlin began to feel mellow. His eyes fell on one girl in particular. She danced wildly between the swirling polka dots of red, green, and blue. She was young. Almost childlike and yet also self-consciously sexy. A sex kitten. A southern California Brigitte Bardot. Whatever happened to Brigitte Bardot, he wondered and ordered another drink.

Somewhere at this very moment, he decided, there was someone wondering whatever happened to Merlin Black. Good question. What *had* happened to Merlin Black? Why had he quit playing, and why was he staging a comeback? Well, as far as the comeback was concerned, the answer was obvious. He needed the fucking money.

His old albums continued to sell moderately well,

especially since his record company had begun to re-issue many of them on CD. But Merlin could not continue to live as he did with an apartment in Manhattan, a house in Malibu, a shrink in Santa Monica, five sports cars, and a considerable appetite for drugs and alcohol.

He could not maintain all this without recreating himself. The Reincarnation of Merlin Black. The Resurrection of Merlin Black. And not the first. By no means, the first. He had more lives than a cat.

He will have to call Peter Pollard to discuss the new band. Find some great, young musicians. It was always the young musicians who kept him alive. Kept him playing new sounds.

Meanwhile the blond, sex kitten continued to dance. Her long hair swayed in one direction as her body swayed in the other. The light show made her movements look jerky, like Charlie Chaplin in an old, silent movie. Merlin chewed on the lemon peel that was twisted and dropped into his drink. It was both sweet and sour. Like the feeling he had watching this beautiful girl dance. A girl too young for him, and of the wrong race.

Not that he was prejudiced against white women. Not at all. There had been that French woman. And now there was Kimberly. Yes, Kimberly. He was more attracted to her than he had ever been to any other white woman. He wished she were here now. If Kimberly were here, he thought, he'd just get out on the dance floor himself and dance with her. He seldom danced unless he was really crocked. He danced with Cheryl in Jamaica on their honeymoon. He can hardly remember a time since. But tonight he was in the mood.

Most of the musicians of his generation couldn't even listen to rock and roll, much less dance to it. Merlin ordered one more drink. There were so many people in this bar. And they all shouted, in order to be heard above the deafening level of the music. The funky bass. The screaming lead guitar. Like it or not, this music was here to stay. If it weren't for him, no one would even listen to trumpets and saxes any more.

"Wanna dance?" Merlin asked the first woman he saw, before he even got a chance to notice what she looked like.

The young white woman, a college freshman, glanced up into the wrinkled face of a middle-aged, black man, whom she had never seen before and who appeared to be stoned.

"No," she said and hurried off to her friends.

"Bitch!" Merlin muttered and stumbled back to the bar. He ordered another drink and downed it quickly. He tried again, but each of the girls, they all seemed so young, turned him down and refused to dance with him. Some were polite. Others turned around to their friends and sniggered. As if the very idea that this old man would want to dance with one of them was so wildly absurd, that it did not even justify a response.

Merlin stormed out of the bar in a huff. There was a time when women, black and white, young and old, had offered themselves to him in the hundreds. He had turned them down in droves every night.

Most of that was because he was either unable or unwilling. He had been unable to have much of a sex life during his heroin years, and he had tried to remain faithful to Cheryl during the decade they were together. He had suffered only a couple of minor lapses. And perhaps one major lapse, toward the end of their marriage. The one with Tara Marlowe.

Merlin went back to his motel room long enough to wash down another tranquilizer with some vodka. He could not even remember the last time he had eaten.

The Eddie Gibbs Quartet was in mid-set by the time he got back to the Lighthouse. Eddie had played alto sax with Merlin back in the 1960's. In fact, as it turned out, everyone in the whole band was a veteran of earlier Merlin Black ensembles.

He recognized all of them. In addition to Eddie, there was Tommy Green on drums, Sonny Potter on piano, and Art McLean on bass. Merlin sauntered up to the edge of the stage and waved to them. They all seemed friendly. All, that is, except Art McLean. There must be some reason for that.

Merlin had the uneasy feeling that there had been some unpleasantness about Art McLean, the enormous man who engulfed his six-foot instrument like an octopus devouring its prey. Art used to play electric, but apparently he had switched back to acoustic.

Merlin found a table and ordered a drink. As Art played his solo, Merlin recalled the unpleasantness. It had been that night at Carnegie Hall in April of 1968, when Merlin's electronic experiment turned into a riot. Merlin had wanted to donate the proceeds to the striking sanitation workers in

Memphis, in honor of Benjamin's untimely death.

What a disaster! he thought. The strike had led to the assassination of Martin Luther King. Merlin's first attempt to sell the public on Jazz Fusion had led to shouting, fist fights, and cops spraying the audience with mace. And just before the band went on stage, Merlin had fired Art McLean, because Art did not want to donate his salary to the striking garbage men.

Well, he himself had been a bit high-handed about it, Merlin had to admit. But, then it was 1968 — the year of causes. Everyone was out of control.

The number ended, and the band received a splattering of applause. Eddie Gibbs approached the mike.

"Ladies and gentlemen, we have Merlin Black in the audience tonight. Merlin, come on up and sit in for a number."

The audience applauded wildly. Everyone turned around and looked at Merlin with surprise and approval.

"Aw no, Eddie. I didn't bring my horn with me."

"I got a trumpet right here. Come on, give us a thrill."

The audience again roared out its enthusiasm. Merlin slowly made his way to the stage. He took the trumpet from the extended arm of Eddie Gibbs. He looked at it dubiously and fingered the valves. He turned his back to the audience and whispered: "Do you know Prince's song 'Little Red Corvette'?"

"No, Merlin," Sonny Potter said. "How about 'But Not For Me', or 'Stranger In Paradise'?"

"Oh, that honky shit," Merlin said.

"Motherfucker probably can't play," Art McLean mumbled.

"What's that, Art?" Merlin asked. "What did you say?"

Art looked Merlin in the face.

"I said, I don't think you still got the chops, motherfucker."

Merlin motioned to Eddie.

"Let's do 'But Not For Me'."

Merlin glanced toward the rhythm section and nodded. Then he turned back to the audience. He put the trumpet to his lips and raised it high in the air. He blew three short notes:

'They're Writ-ing... Songs...' The note began okay but squeaked a little toward the end: 'Of Lo-o-o-ve... But Not For...' Another long note: 'Me-e-e-e...' This time the note shrieked awfully, it farted, totally out of control.

"Told ya the motherfucker had lost his chops," Art muttered.

Merlin stopped playing and pivoted around to the

corpulent bass player.

"What did you say?"

"Nothing. Just play your horn. That is, if you can."

Merlin hurled his trumpet to the floor and sprang on Art. The sound of the cracking of the wooden double bass resonated throughout the bar. It was immediately crushed between the two bodies of the struggling men. Merlin jumped up and wrestled the finger board of the large instrument away from the splintered ruin and the strings of the belly of the bass. He grabbed the piece by the scrolled end and raised it high over the collapsed and reclined body. He brought it down ferociously on Art McLean's head.

Blood spluttered out from the wound that the blow caused on Art's forehead. Merlin lifted the club again, but, before he was able to strike a second time, Sonny Potter leapt off his piano seat and tackled him.

"Twenty years!" Merlin screamed. "Bastard has been after me for more than twenty years."

"Motherfucker is crazy! Certifiable!" Art shouted. "Belongs in the nut house."

Merlin wrestled to loosen himself from Sonny's grasp, as Eddie Gibbs ran to assist in holding Merlin back, and Tommy Green helped Art to his feet.

"Come on," Merlin shrieked. "You want a piece of me. Come on, you big fat tub of lard."

"I'm afraid I'd kill you, Merlin."

"Oh yeah?" Merlin cried. "How come you the one bleeding, motherfucker?"

The amazed and horrified patrons scrambled to get out. The manager called the police. Art McLean broke loose of Tony Green's grasp and rushed over to Merlin, who squirmed under the clasp of Eddie and Sonny.

"You think I give a shit about you, Merlin Black? The best thing that ever happened to me was the night you fired me. You're washed up. A has-been. A nothing. A nobody."

Merlin somehow pulled loose of his captors and swung his fist toward Art McLean's jaw. Art lurched back. Merlin missed, lost his balance, and fell forward to his knees. Art kicked him in the chin, knocking a tooth loose. Merlin felt intense pain, but it only served to make him angrier. He grabbed Art's leg and yanked him down to the floor. He threw himself on the fat man's body. But, before he was able to land a serious blow, Eddie and Sonny pulled him off again.

By then, there were five policemen inside the Lighthouse.

"Okay. Who started this fracas?" one of them asked.

"Merlin Black," Art said, pulling himself up from the floor.

"Which one of you is Merlin Black?"

"Fuck you!" Merlin said and started to walk away.

"Just a minute," the policeman said. "Where do you think you're going?"

"I'm gonna blow this pop stand. I've had enough of this shit."

"Oh no you're not," the policeman said. "Not until I'm through asking you questions."

Merlin reeled around and took a swing at the policeman. The policeman stepped back, but not far enough. The blow landed on his nose. It was not hard enough to do any serious injury, but it was a direct hit. The policeman, stunned, dropped the pad on which he had planned to take notes, and dabbed a handkerchief to his bleeding nose.

"Book him," he shouted. Two of the other policemen yanked Merlin's arms behind his back and handcuffed him.

They dragged him outside and tossed him in the back of the police car. They drove him to the Hermosa Beach Jail, only two blocks away. There, the police took Merlin's wallet, his shoes, his dark glasses, his belt, everything but his t-shirt, socks, underwear, and gaucho pants.

"What choo think I'm gonna do with the shoes, motherfucker? Beat myself senseless?"

The guard refused to answer Merlin's question.

They fingerprinted him and took mug shots. Then they threw him into a small, dark cell. Merlin, suddenly drained of anger as well as energy, simply lay down on his cot.

The tranquilizers clouded his mind. His rage disappeared into a drug-induced trance. He thought about Cheryl. Whenever he was tired or drunk or depressed or weak or sick or lost, he always thought about Cheryl. Only recently Kimberly's face began to appear as well. So different — the two women: one white, one black. They both had those dimples though. And the warm, beautiful smile.

When he got within a block of the building, he saw the removal van. It couldn't be Cheryl, Merlin thought. But it was. Merlin recognized her dark red sofa, as the men carried it down the steps of the gray brownstone and up the ramp into the van.

He had spent the night, or rather morning, in another apartment on the upper east side, not far from the Guggenheim Museum. So he had simply walked the ten blocks south to his own apartment on 79th. He knew that she would be pissed. She had a right to be. He had stayed out all night again.

For the first time since Athens, he had been with Tara Marlowe. But there was no way Cheryl could know that, and besides it hadn't meant anything. In fact, Tara's primary attraction was that she looked like Cheryl. Only he hadn't been able to talk to Cheryl lately. He had been preoccupied with the deterioration of his band. She never seemed to understand his problems. Never took his side any more.

First, John Coltrane had left the band, and then all the others. As soon as he replaced one member, somebody else dropped out. Merlin was at the peak of his popularity, but he could not maintain that peak if he couldn't keep good people in his band. Tara Marlowe had at least listened to him and seemed to understand.

Merlin made his way past the movers who were carrying out a trunk of clothes.

"Cheryl!" he said, as he walked into the open door of his apartment.

"I'll be out in just a few minutes," Cheryl said, as she stuffed lingerie into a suitcase.

Merlin's heart sank, and he knew emphatically that he didn't want to lose her.

"Don't go."

"I'm outta here, Merlin. This is it. I've had it. I've had enough." Cheryl's back was to him, as she pulled more clothes out of drawers and threw them in the general direction of the open suitcase on the bed.

"Cheryl, look at me."

She turned around. She had never looked more beautiful to Merlin. She wore brown, close-fitting slacks and a white sweater.

"I love you," he said.

"You have a funny way of showing it."

"Give me another chance. Please. My new saxophonist is having problems. I was trying to help him."

Cheryl turned back around, wildly stuffing blouses in her suitcase.

"Merlin, I'm not stupid. You've been with a woman. And you're probably shooting heroin again, as well."

"That's a lie," Merlin said. "I haven't used smack for ten years."

Cheryl stopped and turned around. There were tears in her eyes.

"Oh, but you *have* been fucking around."

"No."

"Why should I believe you? Every time you open your mouth you lie."

Cheryl zipped her suitcase and pushed her way past him toward the door. Merlin grabbed her by the shoulders.

She looked him straight in the eyes.

"What? Are you going to hit me again, Merlin? Go ahead. This time I'll call the cops. I mean it."

"No, Cheryl." Merlin dropped his arms to his sides.

"No. I just don't want you to go. We can work it out."

"That's the lyrics to a song by the Beatles, Merlin. It has nothing to do with reality."

"I love you. I'm sorry."

"You're sorry, all right. Now, get out of my way."

Merlin stood aside, and Cheryl walked out of the room. He sat down on the bed and looked around him. All the drawers in the chest of drawers were pulled out. Stockings, underwear, and socks were falling out of them. The sliding closet doors were open. Some of Merlin's suits and a few of Cheryl's discarded dresses were on the floor. The closet was half empty; raped, pillaged, vandalized. Had Merlin come in after Cheryl had gone, he would have thought that they had been robbed.

The bookcases were in a similar condition. There were great gaps between the books and records still on the shelves, and a number of books and LPs lay strewn across the floor.

Merlin put his head in his hands. Why? he thought. How could I have been so stupid? He stood up and walked to the bathroom. He felt like throwing up. His whole body was racked with pain.

He had never experienced true despair until now and he did not like how it felt. It was physical. It was a buzzing in the head, a numbness of the muscles. It was heartburn and a queasy rumbling in the stomach. But most of all it was a profound weariness, a desire to lie down and sleep forever.

Somewhere above the weariness, there were flickers of hope. I'll cling to lies and self-deception, if that's the best I can do, he thought. If that's my only hope. Maybe she'll come back. Maybe she'll change her mind. Maybe she'll realize that she can't live without me. She is flesh of my flesh. Bone of my bone. We are two parts of a single whole. Maybe she'll come back.

And then she did come back. It was not his imagination. It was Cheryl. She had come back to him. And so soon. Only minutes. Although they seemed like hours.

She stood in the doorway of their bedroom and loosened the ring off the third finger of her left hand. She held the diamond up in the air for a second. Looking at it. And then she threw it on the bed.

"There," she said. "I won't be needing that any more. Maybe you can sell it for dope."

Merlin woke up bursting to urinate and with a colossal hangover. Where was he? The tiny cell measured only about eight feet in each direction. The disgusting toilet looked as if it had not been cleaned in years. In fact, the whole cell was rank with the smell of shit, vomit, and piss.

Still, it felt good to empty his bladder. As he aimed his stream into the brownish-yellow bowl, he looked down and noticed blood stains on his black, Billie Holiday t-shirt. And then he became aware of another pain, one in his mouth. He felt around inside and realized that he had lost a tooth.

All his life, Merlin had had nightmares about losing his teeth. He always woke up from these nightmares in a cold sweat, feeling as if something terrible had happened. After regaining consciousness, he would laugh at himself. Why should losing a tooth be such a big deal? But now he *had* lost a tooth, and it *was* a big deal.

It had stopped bleeding, but it still hurt like hell. What had happened to the tooth? He could not remember, but scenes from the previous night began to filter back. He remembered hitting the policeman and getting handcuffed. He remembered attacking Art McLean and destroying the bass. He even remembered the blond sex kitten who danced so provocatively at Pier 66.

Shit, he thought, sitting back down on his cot. I'm gonna have to straighten up my act. That's all there is to it. I must get my shit together for the Hollywood Bowl gig. That will be my salvation. As a man and as an artist. I must make a good impression.

He had pulled it out of the frying pan before, and he could do it again. His career had almost died while he was strung-out on heroin. And again after the riot at Carnegie Hall. He had come back from near-extinction before. He could do it again.

After springing Merlin from the Hermosa Beach City Jail, Kimberly drove him back to the Sea Sprite Motel. Merlin was in a foul temper. He immediately washed down two tranquilizers with more vodka.

"You wanna drink?" he asked.

"Yes. I think I do," Kimberly said. She wore white shorts and a red cotton blouse. The morning was hot and smoggy. Merlin, who sat down by the table at the window, looked up in surprise.

"I thought you didn't drink."

"Yeah, I know. I quit."

"Why?"

"Because I'm an alcoholic."

Kimberly poured herself some vodka from the bottle and put it up to her nose.

"Well, maybe you better not drink it then," Merlin said.

Kimberly bolted back the vodka in one swallow. She made a face and shuddered. Then she slammed the plastic cup down on the kitchen table.

"You've been trying to get me to take a drink since the day I met you. Since the very first conversation we ever had. So, now I take a drink and you start preaching at me."

Kimberly poured herself another vodka and gulped it straight down.

"So you've been trying not to drink?"

"That's right. A.A. The whole routine."

"How long?"

"Five years."

"Five years! You mean you haven't had a drink in five years?"

"That's right."

"Shit, Kimberly, I'm sorry. I didn't know. Why didn't you tell me?"

Kimberly sat down at the table across from Merlin. She moved the vodka bottle out of the way, put her head in her arms, and began to sob.

"Kimberly, don't cry."

"Why not?" Kimberly said, without lifting her head.

"I don't know," Merlin said. "I feel responsible."

"You are responsible, you asshole!"

"Kimberly, look at me."

Kimberly looked up. The tears ran down her cheeks, and her eye make-up was smudged all over her face.

"What's this all about."

"You're the most selfish man I've ever met. Which is probably why I care about you. I've always had atrocious taste in men."

"If you're gonna tell me off," Merlin said. "Then I'm gonna have another drink first."

Merlin poured the last of the vodka in his plastic cup and drank it. "I mean, I got beat up yesterday. Got a tooth knocked out. Spent the night in the Hermosa Beach Jail, which stinks like something outta Mississippi. I guess you might as well finish me off this morning by telling me what a sonofabitch I am. I'd hate to break my losing streak."

Kimberly smiled and stood up. She withdrew into the bathroom.

"Oh, shit!" she said, from there. "My eye make-up is ruined."

"Well," Merlin said. "At least you have your priorities straight."

"Shut up, you bastard." Kimberly came back to the table, holding a wet, baby-blue washcloth to her eyes.

"Are you going to tell me what you're so upset about?" Merlin asked. "Or do I gotta guess?"

Kimberly continued rubbing her eyes with the washcloth. "I'm a writer, Merlin. All my life I wanted to write. You've been so successful for so long, you probably don't even remember what it's like not being a success."

"Oh, I remember, all right," Merlin said. "Just last night I got up on stage and made a fool of myself."

Kimberly pulled the baby-blue washcloth away from her face and stared directly into Merlin's eyes.

"See, there you go. For the first time in our relationship, I try to tell you something about myself. And all you can say is ME-ME-ME. For godssake, Merlin! Give it a rest." Kimberly put the washcloth back up to her right eye.

"I like you this way," Merlin said, both shocked and amused by Kimberly's sudden change in manner. "I always liked my women feisty."

"Like I was trying to tell you," Kimberly continued. "I'm a writer. I've never gotten anything published, except magazine articles. And now I've got this book. You did promise me a credit, right? A 'With Kimberly Gates'?"

"Right."

"Well, I need to remain kinda detached. You know? But then I get all involved with you. You keep begging me to get involved. I'm the one whose gonna get screwed. And I mean in every possible way."

Merlin smiled. "It don't gotta be that way."

Kimberly pulled the washcloth down from her face again and stared him straight in the eyes.

"Well, what are we going to do now?" she asked.

"What do you mean what are we going to do now?"

"We're out of vodka."

"Oh. Well, I'll go get some more."

"Do you need to go to the dentist?" Kimberly looked truly concerned about Merlin for the first time that day.

"Shit, no."

"Sure?"

"I'm sure. Ain't gonna let no goddamn dentist get a hold of me. What's he gonna do, anyway. I lost the tooth."

"I guess you can pass on the tooth fairy, too." Kimberly smiled, showing off her irresistible dimples.

"Tooth fairy! I ain't gonna let no jive-ass, honky tooth fairy in my bedroom, honey. I'll go get that vodka now." Merlin stood up to go.

"No, you won't," Kimberly said. "I'll go. You take a shower. You smell like a horse."

June 30, 1990

Things were happening too fast for Kimberly, spinning totally out of control. Partly, that felt good. She had held herself in, for a long time. She was tired of the price she had to pay in order to remain "in control."

She started up the VW Rabbit and looked around. Hermosa Beach was not that different from her parents' home in Long Beach. It was familiar territory.

She found a grocery store and went inside. She strolled over to the liquor department, on the right-hand side of the store. Rows of alcoholic beverages, lined up in endless succession: whiskey, gin, beer and wine. All the forbidden fruit. Or rather, forbidden fruit juice. Right there in a grocery store.

She knew she had slipped, fallen from her perch of sobriety, as she stared, hungrily, at all that delicious booze. She had begun to drink again, and it felt good. But she knew she could not handle it for long. Well, she would go to confession tomorrow. She could always call up Harvey Wilson, her A.A. companion, and get back on the straight and narrow. Tomorrow. Or later. Maybe, next week.

She picked out a bottle of Smirnoff's vodka and stood in line. She wished, in a way, that she was in love with Harvey, instead of Merlin. Harvey was safe, handsome, reliable, sober. The kind of guy she should be interested in. But there was no passion. And there was no future in the relationship. She just didn't have those kinds of feelings for him.

Her parents would never understand her falling in love with a sixty year old, black jazz musician. She didn't fully understand it herself, except, Harvey was boring. And Merlin was exciting. She wanted to be with Merlin. She preferred to play with the dangerous Merlin Black than to be sober with the safe and serious Harvey Wilson. She would join Merlin and drink with him this one day. She needed a break from her routine, a break from sobriety, a break from respectability.

When she got back to the Sea Sprite, Merlin had cleaned up and was in a much better mood. He took the vodka bottle from Kimberly and poured them both a shot.

"Cheers!" he said.

"L'Chaim," she said, and then drank the liquor. Merlin put

126

the plastic cup down on the table. He caught Kimberly up in his arms and kissed her firmly on the lips. Thin, Caucasian lips, they might be, but they tasted sweet nonetheless.

"Well, I must say, you certainly smell a lot better," she said, smiling.

"Thanks. I'm sorry I was such a jerk this morning."

"Well, Merlin, I suppose it's understandable," she said. "You had a rough night."

"Let me make it up to you."

"What do you have in mind?"

"Food. Lunch. Brunch. Whatever?"

Kimberly smiled again. "You sure know the way to a girl's heart." Then she kissed him, and he held her in a tight embrace for a long time.

"I love you, Kimberly Gates."

"Do you?" she asked, playfully, coyly, coquettishly, as she pulled away from his embrace.

"Yeah. Do you love me?"

"I'll tell you over lunch. Did you say we were going to Chasen's? You promised me Chasen's a long time ago, and we haven't been there yet."

"Well, Miss Gates… You're wearing shorts. Which is fine, because you have sensational legs."

"Thank you," Kimberly said and gave him her best mock-curtsy.

"But you are, nonetheless, wearing shorts, and I'm wearing a t-shirt. When I take you to Chasen's, we'll get dressed to the nine's."

Kimberly poured more vodka in their cups.

"You're just leading me on, Mr Black. You're never going to take me to Chasen's. I do believe you are a deceitful scoundrel and a scallywag to boot." She batted her eyes, doing her very best Scarlet O'Hara. Merlin had never seen Kimberly so funny. But then he had never before seen her after she'd been drinking.

"So, where are we going?" she asked. "McDonald's?"

"Naw. McDonald's! Shit! That's quite a jump from Chasen's to McDonald's. How about McChasen's for some McCaviar?" Merlin laughed. The prince of darkness laughed out loud. In fact, he could not stop laughing. Kimberly laughed too. Merlin could not remember the last time he had laughed, but now he couldn't stop. He was consumed with explosions of guttural laughter that eventually became painful. His sides hurt and the tears rolled down his face.

"I know a place down on the pier," he said, after he finally got control of himself. "The Redondo Beach pier. There's an Indian restaurant down there. It's not Chasen's, but it's pretty good. What do you say?"

"I say 'yes'."

***

Merlin took off his sun glasses and stared at Kimberly across the table. Kimberly was studying the menu. Their table overlooked the ocean. It was a beautiful day. The coastline was visible from Palos Verdes in the south to Malibu in the north. Gentle, white foaming waves rippled just beneath their feet.

Kimberly peeked out from the side of her menu and looked at Merlin, who was grinning from ear to ear.

"What?" she asked.

"Well, when are you going to tell me?"

"When am I going to tell you what?"

"That you love me."

"Pretty sure of yourself, aren't you?" she said and returned her gaze to the menu.

"No." He said it simply, almost as if he were hurt.

Kimberly put the menu down on the table. She looked him straight in the eyes, an act she seldom performed, because he was usually wearing sunglasses. The brown, soulful eyes seemed to reveal such a depth of pain, that it was not really surprising that he so often kept them hidden.

"I love you, Merlin Black," she said, simply and sincerely.

Merlin smiled and picked up his martini. He drank it down in one gulp.

"You're the best thing that's happened to me in a long time."

"You mean since Cheryl?"

"Maybe. You sound jealous."

Kimberly took a sip from her martini. She set it back down on the table and smiled at Merlin.

"I'm not. I'm actually very flattered."

He unbuttoned her blouse and slipped it off her arms. She was not wearing a bra. Merlin discovered that her breasts were firm and lovely, but her skin was so white, so pale. He held his arms up straight, as she slipped off his t-shirt. She kissed his right nipple and continued to stroke it with her tongue. Merlin felt his penis jerk toward erection.

He led her toward the bed. Then he sat down on the side and unzipped her white shorts. Together they tugged and pushed them to the floor. After he pulled down the black lace panties, he marveled at the redness of her pubic hair and the contrast it made with her alabaster skin.

He caressed her buttocks, the soft pillows of flesh, and drew her even closer to him. His hand touched the downy hair between her legs, and then he kissed her there. His tongue explored the soft pedals and deep recesses of her sex, until she purred, until she moaned with pleasure.

They fell on the creaky, queen-sized bed. It was covered with a light-blue blanket. His blackness melted into her whiteness. He raised up on his arms, as if doing a push-up, and then looked into her face.

Her hair, pushed back behind her ears, glowed with a light perspiration. She smiled. Her dimples were wide rivers. Her face seemed fuller than usual, rounder. She looked different. He did not have to be told that this was good for her, that this gentle embrace was no mistake. He did not have to be told that, at this very moment, she was happy.

***

Later, they got dressed. They drank vodka all the rest of the day and walked in the warm sunlight. They swam and ate and laughed and played. They relaxed on the beach. Merlin spread out a beach towel and lay down on it. Kimberly was not his type, he thought. But it felt good being with her. It felt good, too, lying in the warm, open air. Love's silliness was the only thing that really mattered, the only true sanity. He put his hands behind his head, smiled, closed his eyes, and went to sleep.

Kimberly sat next to him in a beach chair, thinking similar

thoughts. Merlin was certainly not what she was looking for. Not only was he major trouble, but she had a great personal need *not* to get involved with him. The chance to write his autobiography, and he had promised her a byline, was the chance of a lifetime. She didn't want to blow it. She needed to keep a professional distance.

But she also knew that love had a sense of humor. It laughed at its victims, when it lifted them up to the skies, and then again when it hurled them down into the abyss of despair. So it had always been with her, but she wasn't ready to give up trying. She was in love with Merlin. You had to take it where you found it, she thought. There was no point in running away from it, or from Merlin, any longer.

Later that night, they returned to the room. They made love passionately, athletically. After resting and cleaning up, he took Kimberly to Pier 66. They did not go to the Lighthouse.

They danced and drank and laughed. The prince of darkness laughed more that night than he had in years, decades. He looked around for the sex kitten, but she wasn't there. He no longer really cared. Merlin wished that Kimberly had come down the night before. He could have avoided a nasty scene, not to mention, losing a tooth. What a difference one night could make! Last night, he had been in despair. Tonight, he was in heaven.

Later, they walked in the sand and held hands. The moon was almost full over Hermosa Beach, and the stars were brilliant. Merlin took off his shoes and walked in the foaming surf. Kimberly held his hand but walked higher up in the sand where the water would not touch her feet. She too was happy. Life was good. The world seemed to be full of infinite possibilities.

Peter Pollard leaned on the bar, tapping his foot. He couldn't believe his ears. It was only the second day of rehearsals at Merlin's Malibu house, and already the band was jumping. The musicians had been *his* a little over twenty-four hours ago, but now they were Merlin's.

He had started the band because he believed that Merlin had permanently retired. He remembered vividly that day, five years earlier, when he had to break the news to Merlin of Cheryl's suicide. He had not realized, even vaguely, how much Cheryl still meant to Merlin at that late date. They had been divorced for twenty years. Merlin never talked about her, but then Merlin rarely talked about the past.

First, there had been the call to Merlin's house. Finally, he had driven over to Malibu to find Merlin naked among the broken shards of a vodka bottle and a sea of his own blood.

Merlin had started off yesterday trying to play rock and roll tunes. He was partial to songs by Prince and Otis Redding. But that had all changed now.

Bearded, athletic Marius Richards and his drum set occupied one corner of the living room. Marius hammered out a steady beat. Valerie Richards, her long blond hair tied in a ponytail, was the least comfortable on the electric organ. She normally played acoustic piano and was still finding her way. Chester Shaw, a large black man with puffy cheeks, stood between Marius and Valerie, pumping out a walking electric bass line.

Tall, skinny Jafar Ali, in front of the rhythm section, teased an insinuating, exotic wail from his soprano sax. Alex Cleaver, a white man in his forties with long grayish-yellow hair, played a dissonant, barking Jimi Hendrix-style solo.

Merlin no longer tried to compete with his younger musicians. His band members, especially Jafar Ali and Alex Cleaver played loud, screeching, and brassy. Merlin's solos were soft and low voltage. He had begun to experiment with a style that remained within his now limited range. The sound wavered. But he made the most of the wavering.

The rest of the band became merely an elaborate rhythm section. Merlin's solo cried out from some painful spot within him. It was not the lyrical, romantic sound for which he was best known. Nor was it the loud Jazz Fusion of more recent years. It sounded like the soft but steady scream of a tortured soul in hell. A scream that did not have to be deafening. At times, in fact, it was barely audible.

Peter thought that Merlin was still trying to regain his chops. That soon he would return to something familiar. But Merlin never merely repeated the glories of his past. If he could play neither loud rock and roll nor lilting, romantic ballads, he would put his liability to its best use. He would announce his pain from a new horn, a horn that blew life into even faltering, tentative notes and gave them a voice that no one had ever yet heard.

Peter should have known better than to doubt his old friend. Merlin could do anything, if he really wanted to. But why, now, all of a sudden, after so long, did he want to? Whatever it was, it seemed to be good for Merlin. He hadn't been this happy or energetic for years.

Kimberly didn't seem that happy. She was nervous and jumpy. And she was drinking heavily. Merlin's appetite for booze and drugs was legendary, but he had never yet been seriously involved with a woman of similar predilections. He had never been involved with a white woman before either, but Peter was not one to make much of that.

Kimberly was sitting now in the corner of the room, with a drink in her hand, and a sour expression on her pretty face. Something in her dimples and her smile, on those rare occasions when she did smile, reminded Peter of Cheryl.

It had been no mistake, Peter thought, that Merlin had risen like a phoenix when Cheryl came into his life.

Merlin had arrived in New York, a kid with talent and boundless ambition. He had gone right up to Charlie Parker, then the hottest name in jazz, and asked to play with him. And asked him too to explain *how* he played. A total stranger. And just a baby, fresh off the train from Memphis.

Parker just smiled and invited Merlin to play with him at Minton's up in Harlem. Course Merlin didn't know that Bird was a junkie, and that all he wanted was money for his heroin habit.

Even after Bird ripped him off several times, Merlin had just sailed over all the shit, till he crashed. That's the way Merlin was, like a high-priced sports car that took off like a bat outta hell, never looking back, never asking questions. Until he ran out of gas. And then he just crashed.

And stayed crashed, until some miracle filled him up with gas again. He had only two speeds. Either full tilt, flat out, gas-pedal-to-the-floor, hundred-mile-an-hour. Or dead still. There was never any half way for Merlin.

He had crashed in the early 50's, a bum, a derelict, playing penny gigs for smack money. Until Cheryl loaded him up again. That drive seemed like it would last forever. It even survived the divorce and the long, rocky marriage to Tara. But it had not survived Cheryl's suicide.

"Merlin, when are we going out to eat?" Kimberly asked.

Merlin had just taken a break, while Jafar Ali soloed again, this time on tenor.

"Later, babe. Can't you see we're really cooking, now? The shit is really coming together."

"I'm hungry. And besides, you were supposed to give me another interview tonight."

"Be reasonable, baby."

"Don't call me, baby." Kimberly got up out of her chair in a huff and went back behind Peter to the bar. She threw a couple of ice cubes in a glass, with a vengeance, and poured straight vodka on top of it.

"Kimberly, don't get drunk," Merlin said.

She stared straight at him. Her eyes flashed what looked like pure and intense hatred.

"That's pretty funny, coming from you."

"Well," Merlin said. "I'm living proof of the evils of drugs and alcohol. Learn from my mistakes."

Kimberly turned to go into the bedroom. "Yeah, well, I think I'd rather learn from my own."

This all had a familiar ring to Peter. Kimberly was like Cheryl, who had once been young and sweet. Merlin was like a vampire. He seemed to suck his energy from women. He became stronger as they become weaker. He took their love and turned it into music. But the women wasted away, as Merlin took, and gave nothing in return. At least not to them. He gave it all to his music.

Maybe Tara Marlowe understood that. She was the only one of Merlin's women who had fought back, who refused to let Merlin suck her vitality out of her. Cheryl had been a dancer, who gave up dancing shortly after they got married. Kimberly was a writer, who seemed to be losing her grip. But

Tara, the actress, had fought Merlin every step of the way. And her career had flourished.

"Peter," Merlin said. "What do you think? What's missing here?"

"Well, Merlin, I like it." Peter crossed over to where Merlin was standing, next to Kimberly's vacated chair. "I like what you're doing. Maybe we could bring down the bass and the organ a little bit during your solo. You're getting drowned out. Course, I realize your living room isn't the Hollywood Bowl."

"Yeah, I've got that little mike too," Merlin said. "You know, the one that fits right down on the bell of the horn? That will definitely amplify the sound."

"Yeah. Okay. But I still think there's too much contrast between your very introspective solo and their sorta breezy, sorta by-the-numbers accompaniment."

"Well, shit, Peter. You know these guys better than I do. Tell 'em how to do that."

"Okay. Valerie...?"

"Yeah, Peter," she said. "Too much?"

"Yeah. A little too much and a little too straight. This is jazz. Mix it up a little bit. Give it a little Herbie Hancock. A little McCoy Tyner."

"Okay," Valerie said, beating out a more sweet-and-sour, complex and subtle pattern. "Like this?"

"Yes," Peter said. "That's more..."

Kimberly stormed out of the bedroom with her handbag and overnight case.

"Babe," Merlin said. "Where ya' goin'?"

"I'm outta here, asshole."

Merlin put down his trumpet and followed her to the back door. "Don't go."

"Why not?" Tears rolled down Kimberly's cheeks. "What good am I doing here?"

"You're doing good here, 'cause I need you. Look at me."

Kimberly turned around and looked at Merlin. He was not wearing his shades.

"I'm going home, Merlin. Don't try and stop me."

"Okay. Go get some rest. I'll call you later, and we'll get some dinner. Okay?" Merlin opened the door for her.

"Yeah, right. If I don't get a better offer first." She rushed out and slammed the door shut behind her.

Kimberly opened the door of her Mar Vista apartment, threw the car keys on the coffee table, and dropped head first on her cheap, black sofa. She had had the same apartment for five years, ever since she left Michael. Its chief virtues were that it was close to the UCLA campus in Westwood, and that it was reasonably far away from her parents shack in Long Beach.

It had been a house at one time, but now it was divided into three apartments. Hers was on the ground floor and included a long living room and two bedrooms. The second bedroom she used as a study, a place for her writing.

Kimberly lay immobile for about five minutes, not wanting to get up. But when the phone rang, she decided to answer it. The phone was in the kitchen, but she managed, by hurrying, to pick it up on the third ring.

"Kimberly, this is Harvey."

"Hi, Harvey."

"I've been calling you for days."

"I'm sorry, I've been out."

"Want a lift to the A.A. meeting tonight?"

"No, Harvey. I'm not going."

"Oh? Anything you want to talk about?"

"No. This isn't a good time for me, Harvey. Can I call you back later?"

"Sure. But…"

"Tomorrow. Okay?"

"Okay."

Kimberly hung up the phone. She pulled a vodka bottle off the shelf next to the refrigerator, unscrewed the top, and drank straight from the bottle.

She carried the bottle with her as she strolled into her study. It was a wreck. Her IBM PC was the one coherent point around which the chaos flowed. There were books, magazines, computer discs, LP sleeves, CDs, tapes, coffee cups, Diet Coke cans, and cereal bowls strewn across the room like the wreckage left after a flood or an earthquake.

The *Playboy* interview was finished, but it would not appear until the November issue. Still that was an accomplishment, at least. The biography, her biography, although it would be called Merlin's autobiography, was another story. She had written long stretches of it. She had labored over it, sometimes into the early hours of the morning. But still there were enormous gaps.

Kimberly sank down into the one comfortable chair in the room and surveyed the flotsam and jetsam, the debris of her life. She took another long swig from the Smirnoff bottle and placed it on the side table. Kimberly knew that she was upset. Very upset. But she did not, herself, fully understand why.

Partly, she'd begun to drink again. After five years of hard work, she had relapsed. She had "slipped," as they say in A.A. It felt more like a head-over-heels tumble, rather than a mere slip. She'd been drinking heavily for a month and a half.

Why was she doing it? To keep up with Merlin? If anything Merlin had slowed down. Especially since he'd gotten serious about his music. Why then had she sped up? Was it like there was a certain amount of drinking the two of them had to do? And if Merlin slowed down, she had to rush in and fill up the gap? Hardly. That was a truly absurd notion. Kimberly took another swig from the bottle.

What then? Merlin had made her aware of how starved she was. Not for food, but for life. Here he was, this genius, who had already done five times as much as most people ever dreamed of. It was the music, the creativity, the accomplishments that she envied. But even more it was the drama. His entire life seemed to be lived out on such a gigantic scale. And she had a little Journalism degree from UCLA, a broken marriage, a boring ex-boyfriend (who didn't even know he was an "ex" yet), and a career that was perpetually stalled at the starting gate of success.

Did she really love Merlin? Yes. But it was partly the Merlin of her own creation. She had fallen in love with the subject of her book. Her book, which seemed abandoned, now that Merlin had begun rehearsing his band. There was so much of it written that she could taste it, could envision the final product. But then, there was so much still left to do.

She felt abandoned by Merlin, both as her lover and as the subject of *her* creative endeavors. Before the rehearsals began, she had had all of him. She had, in fact, more of him than she knew what to do with. They would work ten hours a day. She would come home exhausted, but, nonetheless, would write for hours. And then he would call her again to tell her some tidbit or to invite her out.

But now, Kimberly felt guilty about *feeling* abandoned. Merlin had given her his complete attention, while he was depressed. Now he was busy doing the thing he did best — making music — and he seemed happy. She was glad for him. But now she was the depressed one.

She wanted more of his time, both personally and professionally, and she really didn't know where one ended and the other began. She had a long list of questions to ask him, but he no longer seemed to have any time to answer them.

The phone rang again. Kimberly picked up the vodka bottle, walked back to the kitchen, and answered it.

"Kimberly?"

"Hi, Merlin."

"Are you okay?"

"Define 'okay' "

"Okay enough to have dinner with me?"

"Sure."

"Do you feel up to driving over here?"

"No."

"All right, I'll send a cab."

"All right," Kimberly said, as she took another swallow from her bottle.

"Good. I know a little fish restaurant down on the beach. Sound good?"

"Yeah, fish sounds good. But Chasen's sounds better."

"It's too late for Chasen's. You have to make reservations early."

"Okay. Fish it is."

"Solid! About an hour?"

"An hour's good. I need a shower anyway."

"And Kimberly…"

"What, Merlin?"

"Bring the tape player, if you want."

***

Later, after they'd eaten, Merlin and Kimberly came back to his apartment.

137

"All right," Merlin said, pouring them both a vodka on the rocks. "Fire up that tape recorder and ask me some embarrassing questions. Go on, sock it to me."

"Okay." Merlin's living room was still full of musical instruments. Kimberly made her way through the forest of drums, guitars, and keyboards and found a seat. She pulled her glasses and a small note pad out of her purse.

"I had some questions I wanted to ask you. Lesssee... Oh, yeah. Tell me more about your relationship with your mother." Kimberly flicked on her black, miniature tape player.

"My mother was a scary person. You have to understand, I grew up in a black family in the south, back in the dark ages. I was lucky. Luckier than most, I guess. My father was a lawyer. That made him a member of the black elite in Memphis." Merlin paused and took a swallow from his vodka.

"How am I doing?"

"Great," Kimberly said. "Keep going."

"Well, in some ways, things are worse today. The black kids growing up in the inner cities now. I mean, the conditions are terrible. But in other ways, things are better. I mean my father lived on the edge. He wasn't no Medgar Evers exactly, but he was one of the Top Niggers in Town. You know what I mean? And he was outspoken. He wasn't no 'Uncle Tom'. He told it like it was. The white motherfuckers could have shot him or dragged him off in the middle of the night. The threat of violence was always there. And he had a temper. He couldn't afford to let it get out of hand in public. But when he came home, he'd slap us all around a little. I mean, it was common in those days, you know? Well, my brother..."

"You never mentioned a brother before. I thought you were an only child."

"No. Reed. He died when I was five. He was two years older than me, so I hardly remember him. But the best I can tell, he was kinda sickly. Polio, I think it was. My father slapped him once or twice, and he died. Now, from what other folks tell, it was just an unhappy coincidence. My father didn't kill Reed. But my mother believed that he did."

"I was wondering when you were going to get around to your mother."

"She was ambitious and high-strung. Nowadays, she'd have had a career, you know?"

138

Merlin stood behind the bar. Kimberly came over and picked up the vodka bottle. She filled up Merlin's glass and took the rest back with her. She drank directly from the bottle as Merlin talked.

"But in those days the wife of a lawyer didn't work. She stayed home like a lady. But mama was smart. She had all this ability. She was musical. Played the piano. It's mainly from her I get my musical interest. But she was frustrated. She wanted more out of life. You sure are drinking that shit fast."

"S'all right," Kimberly said. "If I forget anything you say, it'll be recorded here on the tape."

"Anyway, my mother… I really think she hated my father. She didn't have the guts to walk away. That was hardly ever done in those days. It was like an admission of failure, or something."

"Still is with my parents," Kimberly said.

"So she started to drink. And that made her crazy."

" 'Crazy', how?"

"Well, she did shit that she wouldn't have done otherwise."

"And you, Merlin. Does booze make you do things that you wouldn't do otherwise?"

"Yes."

"Then why do you drink?"

"I drink to blot out the shit I don't want to think about. It makes me numb. Why do you drink?"

"I'm doing the interviewing here."

"Okay. Ask me something else."

"Is that all about your mother?"

"All I want to say."

"But there's more, isn't there? There's something you're not telling me. Isn't there?"

"Some things are personal."

"Of course, they're personal, Merlin. Autobiographies are personal. We got to give 'em some dirt, if we want to sell copies."

"Ask me something else."

"Okay." Kimberly looked down at her notes. "Oh, yeah. There is something else. When was it you and Tara Marlowe got divorced. I never found that date."

Merlin took another sip from his drink. He hadn't budged

from behind the bar.

"We didn't."

"I beg your pardon?"

"We never actually got a divorce."

"You and Tara are still married?" Kimberly, who had been getting thoroughly drunk, suddenly sobered up. She hadn't yet given much thought to marrying Merlin. But she was considerably disturbed to learn that he was not single.

"Technically," he said.

"Technically?"

"Yeah. Tara was pressing me hard to get a divorce about the time Cheryl committed suicide. I went into the hospital and just forgot about it."

" 'Just forgot'?" Kimberly tried to hold back her rage.

"Well, I had other things on my mind. Like getting a hundred stitches in my body and trying to decide, if I wanted to go on living. Then Tara moved in with Harry Belafonte. He's married too and doesn't particularly want to get a divorce. So they're living together. And neither Tara nor I felt strong enough about it to press the issue."

Kimberly picked up the vodka bottle and bolted out the sliding glass door. She walked out on the beach toward the Pacific Ocean. Merlin came right behind her.

"What's wrong?" he asked.

" 'What's wrong'? I've been sleeping with a married man. That's what's wrong!"

"Would you mind passing that bottle over this way?"

The night was sultry. The moon was not as full, and the stars were not as bright as they had been in Hermosa Beach. But it was still a beautiful night. The only sound was the swooshing and the flapping of the waves.

"You want me to get a divorce?"

Kimberly stopped and looked at him. His face was ravaged. It was no longer the handsome face of his youth. But it still had enormous character. The sensual lips. The high cheek bones. The nose, wide but straight. And those deep, penetrating eyes. She took the bottle back and drained it of the last few drops of clear, fiery liquid.

"Fuck me," she said.

"Right here on the beach?"

"Yes, right here on the beach."

140

Kimberly stood in Merlin's, creamy tan, tiled shower, letting the warm water massage her all over. She was aware that a lot of sand was coming off her body and accumulating on the floor of the large, luxurious shower room.

She was aware that she was about to get dressed to go out to eat. Merlin was finally taking her to Chasen's. She had heard of this exclusive restaurant in West Hollywood all her life. A place redolent with glamour and history. Where F. Scott Fitzgerald met Sheila Graham. Where Alfred Hitchcock had dined. And Gary Cooper and Henry Fonda, Mae West and Cary Grant. Elizabeth Taylor had spent a fortune flying Chasen's famous chilli from California to Europe in order to seduce Richard Burton, during the filming of *Cleopatra*. Obviously, it had worked.

Kimberly had tried to get her husband, Michael, to take her there, but he had refused.

"Fifty dollars for a bowl of chilli?" he said. "No way."

Kimberly was excited about going out, but she felt groggy and, more than a little concerned about her loss of memory. Most of the day was a blur. She vaguely remembered making love to Merlin on the beach last night but could not remember coming back to his house. She remembered waking up with a terrible hangover and drinking Bloody Mary's in order to feel better. She remembered putting on a bathing suit and going, by herself, to the beach but not much else. She must have passed out on the beach. Too much, she thought. I'm drinking too much.

She dried off and looked at herself in the mirror. Needs some work, she thought. Needs some serious work. She had left a glass of vodka on the sink. She took a sip of it and plugged in the hairdryer.

Merlin opened the door to the room and grabbed her by the waist.

"I was afraid you had drowned," he said.

"Not from without," she said. She put the hairdryer back down and turned around to kiss him. He smiled. That smile. That rare Merlin Black smile, that made up for all the cynicism and bitterness that came out of his customarily unsmiling mouth.

Kimberly remembered what she sometimes forgot: that for Merlin, meaning and truth were relative. Style was everything. This man was some kind of conjurer. Some kind of Svengali. He had hypnotized her with those dark eyes. She cared not what the future held. Merlin was in control. She was his prisoner, and she would not have it any other way.

"You seem happy," she said.

"I am," he said. He kissed her softly on the lips. "What's that mean?"

"What's what mean?" she asked.

"About not drowning 'from without'."

"Oh nothing. Did I have a good time today?"

Merlin pulled back and looked at her. He knew what she meant, but he was not going to say it.

"You got to ask?"

"I feel a little spacey," she said.

"Okay. I'll go cancel that appointment at Chasen's."

"Don't you dare."

"We're gonna be late, anyway. You takin' so much time in the bathroom."

She smiled back at him and took another sip from her drink.

"Well, if you're in such a hurry, why are you in here, bothering me?"

"Okay. I get the message. But the limousine will be here in fifteen minutes."

Merlin shut the door and left Kimberly to finish getting dressed. He walked into the living room, which was still cluttered with musical instruments: drum sets, keyboards, and guitars. He went to the bar and poured himself a vodka, straight up, then walked over to the stereo. He looked through the CDs. Every time his record company re-issued one of his albums on CD, they sent him a copy.

Merlin was not much of one to listen to his old music. He always concentrated on the present. Even during his five year sabbatical from work, he listened primarily to new stuff from other people.

But now his eye caught one of his most popular recordings, one that had been first issued in the 1950's. He pulled the disc from the plastic cover and set it inside the sliding CD drawer. Soon the smooth, romantic melody of "Stranger in Paradise" filled the house.

Merlin had not listened to this in decades. It was a little creepy, like *deja vu*, like remembering something from a previous life. It was almost as if someone else was playing it. Kimberly loved this song. So had Cheryl.

Merlin went back in the bedroom and threw off his black, terry-cloth robe. He pulled out the frilly, white shirt with the French cuffs, that he had worn to Spago's, and slid into it. But for Chasen's, he would wear his tuxedo. He hadn't worn a tuxedo in years.

The disc had ended by the time Kimberly emerged into the living room. She wore a long, glowing scarlet, silk-like dress with a deep V-neck and thin straps which criss-crossed in the back. Her hair, which looked orange, compared to the dress, fell loosely at her shoulders.

"You look sensational," Merlin said, stepping up close in order to peck her briefly on the lips.

"Thanks. You look like you just stepped off the cover of *GQ* yourself, Merlin Black."

"Actually, I *was* on the cover of *GQ* once."

"I know."

***

"Bring us a vodka martini," Merlin told the waiter, once they were seated in their red leather booth.

"Make mine a double," Kimberly said.

"Well, did you spot any movie stars when we walked in?" Merlin asked, as he gazed around the mirrors and brown, wood panelled walls of Chasen's.

"No. Just a famous jazz musician."

"Yeah? Who? Wynton Marsalis?"

"No. Merlin Black."

"Oh! That old goat. You mean he's still alive?"

"Very much alive. Rumor has it that he frolics with beautiful, young redheads on the Malibu beach in the middle of the night."

"Naw! That old fart? You mean he can still get it up?"

The waiter brought the drinks. Kimberly ordered a second double, before he had a chance to leave.

"Well, Miss Gates, Kimberly," Merlin said, lifting his glass in a toast. "I have something to announce."

Kimberly pulled the two olives, skewered on a pink, plastic toothpick in the shape of a sword, from her drink.

"Don't tell me you're pregnant," she said. She clinked the round bottom of her glass to the side of Merlin's and poured the martini down her throat in a single swallow.

"Pregnant? Shit! No, I called up my lawyer today, while you were... sleeping on the beach."

"Passed out on the beach, you mean?"

"Whatever."

The waiter brought Kimberly her second drink.

"Waiter," Merlin said. "Bring us some caviar and a seafood appetizer."

"Yes, sir," he said and walked away.

"Trying to sober me up, eh?" Kimberly drank deeply from the martini. Her pupils were dilated, and her green irises danced wildly in her eyes.

"Kimberly, I'm trying to tell you something."

"Well, just spit it out, Merlin. Stop beating around the bush."

"I started divorce proceedings today against Tara."

"That's great, Merlin. But, you know what?"

"What, Kimberly?"

"I don't feel so good."

"You just need to eat. What have you eaten today?"

"I don't remember," she said, finishing off her martini.

"And stop drinking."

The waiter brought the caviar and seafood appetizer. Kimberly's face turned as green as her eyes.

"Merlin, excuse me. Please." She got up and dashed toward the ladies' room.

Merlin parked the Jaguar in the lot and walked around to open the door for Kimberly. Kimberly sat, staring, not at Merlin, but toward the front, through the windshield.

"Now, tell me again," she said. "Why am I doing this?"

The Betty Ford Clinic is in Rancho Mirage, about a two hour drive from L.A., and about twenty minutes east of Palm Springs on Highway 111. It looks like a country club. The lawn is green, well-manicured, and frequently watered, since it lies in the middle of a desert.

The buildings are made of brown wood and gray steel. They are tasteful and unobtrusive. To the south of the orderly campus stand the majestic San Jacinto Mountains. The air is hot and dry. The desert, sterile and beautiful, stretches out in all directions. Palm trees and lush desert flora enhance the primitive and deadly beauty. It's quiet. After L.A., the quietness can seem overwhelming.

"You're going to dry out here, Kimberly," Merlin said. "While I finish up rehearsals with the band."

Kimberly had been sucking on a vodka bottle since they left L.A. She took a long drink from it now.

"I'm going to miss the concert."

"You need help, Kimberly. Now."

"You just want me out of the way, so you can fuck Valerie, your organ player. How many organs does she play, anyway?"

"I'm not going to fuck Valerie, Kimberly. I love you."

"Yeah, right." Kimberly sipped again from the Smirnoff bottle and made no attempt to get out of the car.

"Come on, Kimberly. Get out."

"In a big hurry to get rid of me, are you?"

"No, I'm not in a big hurry. I love you. I want to marry you. I just thought we could take a walk around, before you check in."

"All right. I seem to have killed this, anyway." Kimberly swirled the last few drops of liquid in the bottle, and then drank them down.

"Do I need my suitcase?"

"No," Merlin said. "We'll come back for it."

They walked around the serene grounds, over bridges, and by small pools. Black and gray ducks scampered out of the pools and onto the sidewalk in front of the pedestrians.

"How come I'm the one checking in, instead of you?"

"How much do you remember about the last couple of days, Kimberly?"

In fact, Kimberly remembered very little. She'd gone back to her apartment for a while on Saturday to work on the book, where she had consumed, at least, a quart of vodka. Merlin had telephoned her in the evening, and she had been wild and incoherent. He demanded that she pack her bags, and she had obeyed.

"Yeah? So, I drank a little," she said.

"A little?"

"Okay. A lot. When did you become such a goddamn saint?"

"I'm no saint, Kimberly. Maybe I'll check in next month."

Kimberly stopped by a wooden bench, beneath an enormous palm tree.

"Why not now, Merlin? Why don't we do this thing together?"

"You know why, Kimberly. I have a gig at the Hollywood Bowl, coming up in four days. I can't back out now. The future of my career rests on this concert. I have to prepare for it."

"Fuck you," Kimberly said. "You're a selfish bastard. Come on, let's get my suitcase. I'm ready to check in."

Kimberly turned back toward the parking lot and took off like a rocket.

Merlin watched her walk away with a combination of sorrow and desire. Her shapely body, inside her red shorts and blue sweatshirt, moved rapidly away from him. He really believed that this was the best thing for her, but he regretted her bitterness. He also regretted that he would not be able to see her for a month, or sleep with her. He could see her only on Sunday afternoons, and then strictly in full view of staff and fellow patients.

"All right, Kimberly. You don't want to stay? We'll drive back to L.A."

"No, I'm staying."

Kimberly halted by the trunk of Merlin's Jaguar, waiting for him to open it. He stood on the other side, with the car key in

146

his hand.

"I thought we agreed. I thought you wanted to do this."

"I do. Now, open up the trunk."

"I'll come down next Sunday to see you."

"Don't bother."

"They won't let me call you. You have to call out to me."

"Don't hold your breath."

Merlin opened his trunk and pulled Kimberly's dark blue, Verdi suitcase out. She picked it up, turned around, and walked away toward the reception building.

"Kimberly, don't go away like this. I love you."

She didn't turn back or say anything. She was scared, angry, and lonely. She knew she could reconcile with Merlin later. She wanted to make her point, now. After all, he didn't have a monopoly on bitterness. She had a fair amount, herself.

She checked in at the reception desk. She had already given them plenty of information in L.A. They assigned her a room in a residential unit for women only. A member of the staff showed her to her building. When she opened the door, a young woman in her mid-twenties was sitting on the opposite bed, reading. She glanced up from her book as Kimberly entered.

"Hi, I'm Alison. Alison Harkins."

Kimberly put down her suitcase and walked over to shake hands.

"Hi. I'm Kimberly Gates."

"Well, welcome to Hell, Kimberly. You're just going to hate it here."

Merlin Black was already thirty minutes late. The ever-calm Peter Pollard was worried.

Valerie Rachel had her long, blond hair done up in Caribbean-style braids. She wore a many-colored seersucker mini dress over a white t-shirt. A smile decorated her round face, but it could not hide her tenseness.

"Is he gonna show, Peter?"

"I don't know, Valerie."

The dressing room was small and windowless. There was coffee, wine, Scotch, and the Wizard's favorite brand of vodka on a table in the corner.

Alex Cleaver's gray-blond hair spread out like a lion's mane. He wore jeans and a purple polo shirt. Tall, lean Jafar Ali wore a tight, black leather pants and jacket outfit. Marius Richards, the drummer, was naked to the waist. His blue jeans had loud yellow and orange patches. The bass player, Chester Shaw, looked formal in his white dress shirt and tan slacks.

"What happens if he doesn't show, Peter?" Marius asked.

"We'll go out there and play ourselves," Peter said.

"Talk about a hostile audience," Chester said.

Valerie poured herself a glass of wine. It was her first.

Merlin burst into the room like a tidal wave. He carried his trumpet case.

"I'm sorry, guys," he said. "I can't do this."

The others shrank before the master. Only Peter dared to stand up to him.

"Of course you can, Merlin."

"Peter, I'm sorry."

"Merlin, sit down."

Merlin obeyed after filling up a plastic cup with *Stoli*.

"What's wrong, Merlin?"

"My mind's not on it, Peter. I'm thinking about Kimberly."

"Merlin, you have to go on that stage. I don't care if you only blow two bleeps from your trumpet. You have to appear."

"Why?"

"For me. For my musicians. They're like my children. If they get a chance to play with you, if only once, it will *make* their career. They can coast for the rest of their lives on having performed with Merlin Black once. Like when you played with Charlie Parker. Remember?"

"Of course."

"You brought your trumpet with you tonight, Merlin. That must mean something."

"It's just automatic. Like locking my car door." Merlin drained his plastic cup and leaned back in the folding chair.

"Will it do Kimberly any good, if you don't play?"

"No."

Peter got down on one knee and took Merlin's hand in his.

"For once in your life, do something unselfish. For me. Your reward will be that you'll make five people, six counting me… Six people very happy. And…" He paused. "And if you don't play, Merlin, I promise I'll never speak to you again."

Merlin looked deep into Peter's eyes, trying to see if he really meant it, or if he was kidding.

"O. K., Peter. I'll do it. For you."

"Great!"

The other five musicians breathed a collective sigh of relief and prepared to go on stage.

"Now, Merlin," Peter said, standing up. "There are three sets of electric keyboards on stage. Valerie will play one of them. One is for you, and I'll plink away at the third one. I also have my flute with me. There's a set of hand drums. Marius can play those. But if you want to keep him on his regular drums, I can play them too. Now, you're in charge. But, if you get tired, just nod to me. I'll take over. Okay?"

"Okay, Peter. But I won't get tired. I'll do it."

"Thanks, Merlin."

"No, thank you, Peter." Merlin got up.

Repeatedly, the MC had assured the audience that Merlin Black was in the house and would soon be on stage. Privately, he wasn't so sure. Finally, Peter Pollard walked up behind him and touched him on the arm.

"Let's go," Peter whispered. "He's here."

The MC hurried to the microphone and introduced the musicians, as each came out on stage.

"Ladies and gentlemen, on drums, Marius Richards. On electric bass, Chester Shaw. On lead guitar, Alex Cleaver. On keyboards, Valerie Rachel. On soprano saxophone, Jafar Ali. On everything imaginable — Peter Pollard. And finally, the star of tonight's show, playing for the first time anywhere in five years, the incomparable Merlin Black!"

The applause deafened Merlin, as he approached the microphone. He felt the heat of the spotlight on his face. He took off his dark glasses and looked out at the capacity crowd that had jammed itself into this enormous amphitheater. He was paralyzed with fear. He wished he had not agreed to do this.

A woman in the front box-seat section with frizzy red hair stared up at him. He thought of Kimberly and wished she were there. He loved her. He would play for her, even though she was not here.

He put his dark glasses on again and turned around, his back to the audience. His fans were used to that. It was practically his trademark. A part of his legend.

He was immaculately dressed, in a stylish black Brooks Brothers suit and a wide silk tie. His brooding round face and angry flashing eyes were hidden now from the audience.

He raised his trumpet toward the ceiling of the giant, arched shell and blew a long, stunning note. The song, "Little Red Corvette," was an attractive ditty. But when it flowed from Merlin's horn, it was re-invented, recreated, born anew. He turned a pop tune into a symphony of love, longing, and loneliness. Bitter and sweet. Bitter-sweet. Like sugar and lemon. Like pain recollected through the cloud of memory. The triviality of life's quotidian, elevated by art to a level of lofty contemplation. Like Michelangelo and Mozart. Like Shakespeare and Tchaikovsky.

Marius Richards pounded a furious beat over Chester's plunking bass line. Valerie and Peter struck long, spacey organ chords, while Alex Cleaver tortured out an angry electric guitar riff. Merlin plugged his trumpet into the electric wa-wa pedal. By inserting and removing his mute over the funky wa-wa twang, he imitated Alex's screeching guitar. Merlin had never made a sound quite like this before. He liked it.

So, apparently did the audience. They sat in rapt awe of an artist, not re-hashing his old hits, not reliving his past glory, but pushing ahead courageously into the future. A genius who reminded them of the beauty of suffering and the awful pain that lay at the core of the human experience. They could barely wait until the song ended, before they were on their feet, screaming and applauding. Merlin turned around briefly and nodded to the audience. He did not smile.

August 24, 1990

Kimberly finished sweeping the sidewalk. That was her duty. Each morning she swept the duck shit off the sidewalk. The Betty Ford Clinic thought that was a good way to build character. They called it "therapeutic duties." It had been the second thing on the schedule each day, right after the meditation walk and right before breakfast.

Great way to work up your appetite, Kimberly thought. Sweeping duck shit.

After breakfast, Kimberly went to the big lecture hall. Betty Ford herself was there. She spoke once a month.

"I want each and every one of you to know," the former First Lady said, "that I have been exactly where you are now. I know exactly how you feel."

I doubt it, Mrs Ford, Kimberly thought. I sincerely doubt it. I guess I should be impressed with your august presence here today. But I happen to be a Democrat. I voted for Jimmy Carter. Maybe I'll appreciate this more, later on.

Kimberly was feeling better now, than she had when she first came here. At least the headaches had lessened. She had slept the first full day she was there, but they had made her participate on the second and every subsequent day. Saturday night and Sunday were the only days the patients had any free time. Every other day was neatly structured and fully supervised. Today was Friday, so she could, at least, start looking forward to her first weekend.

She had not even been allowed to make a telephone call during her first week. She would be able to call Merlin on Sunday. She would not know how the Hollywood Bowl concert went until then.

Kimberly looked around the auditorium for her room-mate, Alison Harkins. She wasn't there. Nor was she at the A.A. meeting which came next. Kimberly liked Alison, even though she was a lot younger. They got along.

They shared a common cynicism about the routine of the clinic. A cynicism that bordered on subversion. Neither was exactly zealous in the pursuit of sobriety. Alison had been forced by her parents, against her will, to come. She was in her third week but hated every minute of it.

151

At night, when they were alone, the two women made fun of everything: the lectures, the food, the 'Twelve Steps', the staff, even the other patients. This made Kimberly feel almost like a teenager at a slumber party. There was nothing sacred, and it was the one part of her day Kimberly truly enjoyed.

"Step One," Granny said. 'Granny' was the female patient chosen by the staff to run the A.A. meeting. "We admitted we were powerless over alcohol — that our lives had become unmanageable."

Kimberly had already heard this stuff so many times — for years at A.A. meetings and at least twice a day since she had been here — that she had memorized it. I guess that's the point, she thought. Keep repeating the propaganda until it becomes subliminal.

"Step Two: Came to believe that a Power greater than ourselves could restore us to sanity."

Kimberly had a hard time buying this God-stuff. She had been brought up in a strict, traditional Catholic manner, and she had eventually rejected it all. If her alcoholic, abusive father was a good Christian, then she would have none of it. In fact, her father was sort of like the paternalistic God of Christianity — cruel, arbitrary, insensitive, and unforgiving. How can you believe in a kind, loving father if you've never had any experience of one?

After lunch, there was group therapy and then another lecture in the big auditorium. Alison did not show up for any of these activities. Kimberly was getting worried, but she didn't want to say anything to the staff. If Alison was up to something, and that was entirely possible, Kimberly didn't want to blow her cover.

The lecturer, a physician, was talking about "Chemical dependency and low self-esteem." And the Twelve Steps. And God, God, God. Kimberly spaced out. She started thinking about Merlin.

She loved him. She missed him. She was dying to know how the Hollywood Bowl gig went, but still she was mad at him, although she was not quite sure why. Maybe she did suffer from low self-esteem. It wasn't the race thing, though, like Merlin kept suggesting. She had never looked down on black people. She had never dated a black man before, but that just proved, to her mind, that it was Merlin himself, and not the idea of some black stud, that appealed to her.

By most definitions, Merlin was the American Dream Come True. He was more than just a success. He had distinguished himself in an artistic and highly competitive field and had triumphed. He was one of a kind. A legend. Practically a national monument.

But then there was the other side. The dark side. Merlin was a depressive, cynical, bitter misanthrope. He pretended to be a racist and a sexist. But Kimberly did not believe he was either. It was a pose, a performance. A part of his legend.

And the drugs. Merlin had survived a lifetime of drug abuse. Did that, in itself, appeal to her? Did that give Kimberly an excuse, a red light, so that she could continue to drink and not worry? She was not sure. She knew that she really was an alcoholic. She had tried to be good. For five years, she had been a good girl. And she had been bored, depressed, a shadow walking through life, not a person truly alive.

Something in her wanted someone to awaken her. The bad girl inside wanted out. Merlin seemed like someone who could let his bad boy come out and play indefinitely. It was, if anything, his genius. He could walk on the edge of self-destruction and never fall over.

And who knew more about Merlin than she? No one. Not even Merlin himself, probably. She was the world's leading expert on Merlin Black. She was his Boswell. And his life was her career. Through him and her book on him, she would fulfill her lifelong desire to be a serious writer.

"The point…" The lecturer's words suddenly dove back into Kimberly's consciousness. "The point is not so much to blame our parents for our lousy childhood, as to recognize that we lack something. Like a vitamin or a mineral. And, like a vitamin or a mineral, this 'something' can be provided."

The speaker, a short, balding doctor in his late fifties droned on and on. Kimberly shifted in her seat and tried to filter him out. She had heard it all before. How we must be responsible. Kimberly was tired of being responsible. She wanted Merlin to take over. She wanted him to show her how to live on the edge. Together they could play. With Merlin, she would not have to be a good girl all the time. She could come alive. She could be herself and not somebody else's idea of acceptable behavior. Alone, she would self-destruct. But with

Merlin, she could walk on water.

Why then was she so bitter? Because he had abandoned her for music. He had left her here to rot. She had accused him of flirting with Valerie, his keyboardist. But it was not Valerie who was Kimberly's rival. It was the music itself.

He had abandoned Harriet and Tara for music. He had neglected Cheryl, who before Kimberly, had been the most important woman in his life. He continued to mourn Cheryl. But if he had the same choice again between music and Cheryl, he would make the same decision. It was the music that made him invulnerable. Without that, he would have died long ago.

He had abandoned humankind for his art. He lived outside the normal world of people, of human relations. And he was fully aware of the sacrifice he had made.

His music was a cold companion on lonely nights, she imagined. But, without it, he would have been nothing. He knew, although he would never admit it, perhaps never could even articulate it. His cynicism was the residue of his sacrifice. What was left over after the human part had been lobotomized. That, and the music itself, which was lonely and sad, but which also had spoken to millions.

After dinner, Kimberly hurried back to her suite to see if her room-mate was there. Alison, wearing blue jeans and a 'Guns N' Roses' t-shirt, danced around the room with a yellow Sony Walkman radio-cassette player plugged into her ears. She was a small woman, really just a girl, about half Kimberly's age, as well as half her size. She was pretty in an undramatic sort of way, with a round, open face, short black hair, heavy eyebrows, and almond-shaped, brown eyes.

"What are you doing?" Kimberly asked, but Alison did not hear her. Kimberly moved into her visual range, and Alison laughed.

"Guess what I've got?" she said.

"What?"

Alison pranced over to her bed and pulled a large bottle of *Absolut* vodka from underneath her pillow.

"Ta-dah!"

"Alison!"

"Want some?"

"Yes. No. What if they catch us?"

Alison screwed off the top and took a long swallow.

"What are they going to do? Throw us out of here? That would be my fondest dream come true."

Kimberly accepted the bottle that Alison offered her and took a swig.

"How did you get this?"

"My boyfriend left me a car." Alison pulled keys out of her purse and jangled them in front of Kimberly.

"A nice, white Toyota Celica. He dropped it off last night in the parking lot and got a ride back to L.A. with his buddy. So, I went out today on an excursion. And I'm going out again tonight. Wanna come?"

Kimberly took another swallow from the vodka bottle and sat down on Alison's bed.

"Gee, I don't know, Alison. Where are you going?"

"Well, we could drive into Palm Springs and have a little party or we could just leave and go all the way back to L.A."

"I don't know." Kimberly kept drinking from the bottle. She was not even thinking about the act or the consequences. She drank automatically, as she always did.

She remembered once asking Merlin if booze made him do things he wouldn't ordinarily do. He had said "Yes," and asked the same question back to her. She hadn't responded, and, even now, did not know the true answer. If she had not begun to drink tonight, would she have decided to stay on at Betty Ford? Or did she really want to leave?

After a short time, it no longer really mattered. The bottle was empty: that was the crucial thing. Given that indisputable fact, there was no longer really any choice. She could stay, lose her best, her only friend at the clinic, and sweep duck shit in the morning with a hangover. Or... or, she could go. Back to life. Back to L.A. Back to Merlin.

The two women repressed their giggles and gathered together a few things. They hadn't consciously decided if they were coming back or not. So they took their toiletry articles and a change of clothes and stuck them in their smallest bag. They stuffed these under their coats and made their way outside. It was not illegal to go outside after hours. And, since it was often cold after sunset in the desert, even in August, they did not look conspicuous at night with their coats on. In fact, escaping was easy.

Patients were not allowed to keep automobiles on the

155

premises. Guards assumed anyone leaving must be a member of the staff.

Alison drove the white Toyota Celica off the campus and past the Eisenhower Medical Center. For a while, they zigzagged through streets named after golfing celebrities — down Bob Hope Drive, past Frank Sinatra Drive and Gerald Ford Drive to Dinah Shore Drive.

As soon as they hit the main highway, they stopped at a grocery store, where they each bought their own private bottle of vodka.

"See if there are any tapes under your seat," Alison asked Kimberly as they got back in the Toyota.

Kimberly pulled out a slim tape case, unsnapped the clasp, and looked at the titles on the sides of the cassettes.

"Got any Merlin Black?" she asked.

"Who? Your old man? He's a musician?"

"Yeah."

"What group is he in?"

"His own group. He plays jazz."

"Jazz? You mean like Kenny G.?"

"No, not exactly. Never mind. What would you like to hear?"

"You know what I want. Guns N' Roses."

Alison drove with her left hand and drank vodka with her right.

"Okay," Kimberly said. She stuck the cassette in the dash player and screwed off the top of her bottle. The vodka tasted strong and warm. Soon the familiar numbness would kick in, and she would feel much better. Or, at least, she would not feel so much.

Axl Rose screeched his message through the car speakers:

> *Welcome to the jungle,*
> *It gets worse here every day...*

***

Joseph and Karen Lee, a Korean-American couple from L.A., were taking their newborn daughter Josie to meet her grandmother, Karen's mother, who had retired to Palm Springs. Highway Ten, the eastern extension of the San

156

Bernadino Freeway, was unusually deserted for a Friday night.

Joseph wasn't crazy about his mother-in-law, but he always enjoyed getting out of L.A. and breathing the clean, desert air. He liked the scenery, odd as it was. In some places, the desert looked like a lunar landscape. No buildings anywhere.

His Chevy Blazer station wagon passed strange windmills. Not like the quaint, friendly windmills of Holland, but eerie, metallic windmills out of some science fiction novel. Scientists must have placed them there to study the stars or to receive messages from outer space. As far as Joseph could tell, they were not attached to anything. He had no idea why they were there or what they did.

The night was clear with a bright, glowing moon, almost full. The stars, miraculously visible, sparkled as they never did in the city. Joseph felt good. He was a father now, the head of a household. He loved his wife, his baby, and his work. Life was good. It was good, too, to be driving, at night, in the desert, along a mercifully, deserted highway.

At first, he was not alarmed when the headlights of the oncoming car swerved back and forth. But then the opposing car, a small compact of some sort, seemed to lose control altogether. The other car veered over into his lane, and the headlights bore down on him.

Surely, the driver will turn back into his own lane, he thought. But by the time Joseph Lee decided to run off the highway and down into the steep ditch, it was too late.

Merlin did not like funerals. In fact, he had only been to two in his whole life: his son, Benjamin's, and Duke Ellington's, a man he greatly admired, but hardly knew. Merlin had not attended the funeral of either one of his parents. Strung out on heroin at the time his mother passed away in a mental hospital in Memphis, he had made no serious attempt to attend the services.

He would not have made it to Kimberly's funeral at Our Lady of Sorrows Catholic Church in Long Beach without the gentle help and assistance of Peter Pollard. Merlin could not yet accept the notion that Kimberly was really dead. He had first heard it yesterday afternoon, less than twenty-four hours ago, but did not yet believe it. He had only just begun to realize that he loved her. *That* had taken long enough to sink in.

He had no idea of the details. Peter had explained them to Merlin. How both the women in the Toyota Celica were killed: Kimberly immediately, Alison, the next morning in the hospital.

The people in the other car, the Korean-American couple and their baby were all critical, but were expected to live. Peter had told Merlin all of this several times. But Merlin hadn't heard. He knew that something was terribly wrong. But he was not ready to believe that Kimberly was actually dead.

He refused to sit on the front pew with Kimberly's family. He sat rather with Peter in the middle pew on the right side of the center aisle. He was dressed in a white suit and a black t-shirt. He held his trumpet in his lap. He had agreed to play at the graveside.

He heard the priest drone on with the usual stuff: "For God sent not his Son into the world to condemn the world; but that the world through him might be saved. He that believeth not is condemned already... And this is the condemnation, that light is come into the world, and men loved darkness rather than light. Kimberly Gates loved the light. We can be certain of that. She was a lovely and loving woman. A good Christian." The priest walked around the casket now, sprinkling holy water.

Merlin had never met Kimberly's family. He guessed at their identities. On the front pew: her parents, Don and Vivian

158

Gates, her ex-husband, Michael Cook, her sister Natalie, her brother-in-law Jim, her namesake niece Kim, and her nephew Tommy. Merlin remembered Kimberly describing and discussing these people. It was more difficult to distinguish Harvey Wilson, the ex-boyfriend, with whom she had gone to A.A. meetings. It might be the blond guy in the third row. There were only about thirty people there, and he seemed closest to Kimberly's description.

Merlin didn't know what, if anything, they knew about him. But he suspected that they knew little.

They knew that Kimberly had been working with him. That she had been writing his autobiography. But they didn't know that he had been her lover. They had asked him to sit on the front row out of deference to him as a celebrity, but they had no inkling of how close the two had been or how devastated Merlin felt.

The priest led the congregation in the Lord's Prayer. The organist played a lugubrious hymn, and the mourners passed in silence before the open coffin. They knelt and received the Holy Eucharist. Merlin did not move.

"Don't you want to pay your last respects?" Peter asked.

"No," Merlin said. "I want to remember her the way she was." He got up and started to walk out of the church. But after he had taken several steps, he changed his mind and walked up the aisle to the casket.

Kimberly was wearing the blue pastel summer dress that she had worn the day he had taken her to the Hollywood Bowl. Merlin could tell that the mortician had applied heavy makeup to her face. Her skin looked darker than its usual pale self. He could still make out the freckles underneath, even the ones on her lips. The thin lips of her mouth, which had been pulled up into a slight smile, an enigmatic, archaic smile, enough of a smile to indicate the soft line of her dimples. The dimples that always reminded Merlin of Cheryl.

Merlin sat back down. The ushers closed the casket and carried it out. The priest followed behind. Everyone filed out of the church. Merlin was the last one to leave the building.

Kimberly's parents and her sister Natalie rode ahead in the hearse along with Kimberly's coffin. Jim and his two kids, Tommy and Kim, were in the second car of the procession. The man Merlin believed to be Harvey Wilson sat in the front seat of Peter's car along with Peter himself. Merlin got in the back seat alone.

"I've always admired your music, Mr Black," Harvey said, sticking out his hand to shake Merlin's. "Hi. I'm Harvey Wilson." He was an average looking guy, with short, blond hair, a mole on his right cheek, and a long, skinny nose.

"Glad to meet you." Merlin shook the white man's hand. "And thank you."

"I guess you saw more of Kimberly toward the end than anyone," Harvey said. "She was always talking about you."

"Yes," Merlin said. "I guess I did."

"She hadn't started drinking again, had she? She was acting strange there toward the end. I was worried about her."

Merlin, at a total loss for words, stared incredulously at Harvey, who was obviously not well informed about Kimberly's last days.

"I don't... I don't know, Harvey."

Peter's car arrived at the graveside. Other cars came and parked behind them. Merlin and his companions followed the two earlier groups up to the site. A thin stream of people, less than the thirty at the church, gathered around the open grave. Most stood. Only Kimberly's parents were seated.

The priest read again from the scriptures: "I tell you a mystery. We shall not all sleep, but we shall all be changed, in a moment, in the twinkling of an eye, at the last trumpet. For the trumpet shall sound, and the dead will be raised imperishable, and we shall be changed. For this perishable nature must put on the imperishable, and this mortal nature must put on immortality. When the perishable puts on the imperishable, and the mortal put on immortality, then shall come to pass the saying that is written: 'Death is swallowed up in Victory. O death, where is thy victory? O death, where is thy sting'?"

The priest motioned for Merlin to come up, but Merlin, lost in thought, didn't notice. Finally, Peter touched him gently on the arm.

"Merlin, it's time."

Merlin looked at Peter and then at the priest. He walked over to Kimberly's, now closed, casket. He looked down at the casket, silently, for an embarrassingly long time. Then he turned around and faced the mourners — his audience. He looked at Kimberly's parents and pulled, with great effort, the trumpet to his lips.

He played the black gospel, "Take My Hand, Precious Lord." It was a plaintive call for help from the lost and desperate, and Merlin played it beautifully. He played a few suspect notes, but no-one noticed. The feeling, the pain, the loss, all communicated deeply. His were the only dry eyes in the group. He finished on a long, anguished note and moved back to his place among the mourners.

"I am the resurrection and the life," the priest said and sprinkled holy water on the coffin again. The coffin was then lowered into the ground.

"I am the resurrection and the life," the priest repeated. All bowed their heads. "We must not mourn the passing of Kimberly Gates. Not now while the angels are leading her to paradise." The priest crossed over to Kimberly's parents and shook their hands.

The service was over. No one spoke to Merlin. The mourners gave their condolences to Kimberly's family and then began to leave. But Merlin remained, motionless, staring down at his feet, until he heard a voice.

"Thank you so much, Mr Black. That was lovely." Merlin looked up into the face of Kimberly's mother. Vivian Gates was a very large woman. Her husband was supporting her. Whether she was unstable from grief or from her enormous weight, Merlin could not decide.

"You're very welcome, Mrs Gates."

"I have to ask you something else."

"Anything," Merlin said.

"The book. Kimberly's book about you?"

"Yes," Merlin said. "What about it?"

"She put so much work into it. I hope you'll see that it's completed. And I hope that you will give her some credit for it. I'm sure it would make her happy."

"I'll do that, Mrs Gates. I promise."

"Thank you. You're a very kind man."

Vivian Gates waddled off with the help of her skinny husband. Everyone left. Harvey Wilson caught a ride with someone else. Only Peter stayed behind with Merlin. They sat in the chairs vacated by Kimberly's parents. For a long time, they remained silent. The workmen lowered the casket and filled the grave with dirt. Finally, Peter broke the silence.

"Merlin, why don't you stay with us for a while. Maria would love to have you. And your namesake... You know, he idolizes you. He'd be delighted if you stayed with us."

Merlin didn't say anything. He held his trumpet in his lap with his right hand. His gaze still toward the ground.

"What do you say, Merlin?"

"What, Peter?"

"Stay with us for a while? Till you feel better?"

"No. No, Peter. Thanks a lot. But I can't do that. You go on, now. I want to be by myself for a while."

"Merlin, I'm not going to leave you here."

"Go on, now, Peter. I'll be all right."

"How will you get home?"

"I can catch a cab."

"Are you sure?"

"Yes. Please, Peter. Go."

"Okay. Will you call me tomorrow?"

"All right."

"Promise?"

"Yes. Go on, now."

Merlin listened to Peter's soft footsteps as they receded. It's very quiet in Our Lady of Sorrows Cemetery. He saw squirrels, robins, and mourning doves hop and scurry over the small, undulating green hills that stretched out in all directions. He heard crickets and, occasionally, a nut or a twig falling off a tree. In the distance, he could hear the drone of automobiles. They sounded as if they were miles, rather than just blocks, away. Twice, an airplane passed overhead.

Daylight gave way to dusk. Merlin's trumpet slid off his lap and onto the ground. Merlin himself slipped out of the chair and to his knees. He toppled over onto his face and crawled slowly, inching his way with his hands and feet, like a man climbing the sheer cliff of a mountain.

He came to rest on the fresh earth which separated the body of Kimberly Gates from him and from life. He kneaded the soil with his hands like a kitten, too early weaned from its mother, grasping for what was no longer there, but should be.

"God," he moaned. "Why?" He lay face down in the mud, expecting an answer. It didn't come. Long ago he had called on God for help. He was only a child, and he had nowhere else to turn. God, help me. God, I need you. God, where are you?

But his cries were not answered. The silence deafened him and made him hard. So many people found a way to believe. Does God speak to them, but not to me? Is it because God hates me? Why? Why won't he come to me? If not now, when?

God, if you want my guilt, you've got it. Do you want me to take all the blame? Is that it? Okay, I killed Kimberly Gates, the one person I love more than life itself. It's all my fault. Okay? Just talk to me. Tell me you forgive me. Or tell me you don't. I don't care. Just speak to me. You spoke to Martin Luther King. You spoke to Malcolm X. You spoke to John Coltrane and my poor sick mother. Speak to me.

There was no sound but the crickets and the distant roar of traffic. An attendant came up to Merlin.

"Sir, I'm afraid the cemetery is closed."

"What?"

"The cemetery is closed, I'm afraid you'll have to leave."

"Oh."

Merlin got to his feet and walked out of the cemetery. He was half a block down the sidewalk before he missed something he was accustomed to feeling in his hand. His trumpet. He walked back. There was no one around. He jumped the small brick wall and went back to the grave site. Merlin saw the trumpet lying in the dust. He picked it up and started to walk back toward the road.

He passed a large white marble monument: Christ crucified on the cross. At first, he thought nothing of it. Then, in a frenzy of uncontrollable rage, he ran back to the cross and began to beat his trumpet against the white god who had betrayed him.

He hammered away relentlessly, lost in a violent and passionate trance, purging away the pent-up anger and resentment. He hammered away like a sculptor at work, or a convict on a chain gang. He hammered away until the bell of the horn caved in on one side and then on the other. He bent the tubing, until the valves fall off. And the brass that once played incomparable music was beaten and destroyed. The pieces fell to Merlin's feet as worthless litter, refuse, garbage. The white god on his marble cross, however, remained the same — cold, hard, and untouched by Merlin's torment.

"It's perfectly normal," Dr. Russell Dover said, leaning back in his chair. He wore the same serious look as usual, vitiated only by the incongruous W.C. Fields-like, bulbous nose. "It's perfectly normal in situations like this to blame yourself. We all want to take responsibility for things that are out of our control. It helps us to make sense out of a senseless tragedy. We want life to be logical, even if we have to blame ourselves in order to force logic on the chaos of events. In what sense do you think you are to blame for Kimberly Gates' death, Merlin?"

"I made her go to the clinic."

"The Betty Ford Clinic?"

"Yes."

"Why did you do that, Merlin?"

"Because she was drinking more and more every day. She was totally out of control. I was afraid that she was going to kill herself."

"So you were doing the right thing for Kimberly?"

Merlin had not slept. His mind was foggy, making it difficult to put his thoughts into words.

"There were other reasons."

"Such as?"

"I was trying to get my band together. To stage my comeback at the Bowl. She was always bugging me to do interviews. I wanted her out of the way for a while."

"What was Kimberly to you, Merlin?"

"I love her. Loved her. No, goddamn it! I still love her."

"Your mother was an alcoholic, too, wasn't she?"

Merlin jumped out of his seat.

"Fuck you and your Freudian bullshit! You think I don't know what you're driving at? You think the dumb nigger doesn't get what you're driving at?"

"Why are you so angry, Merlin?"

Merlin sat back down again and put his face in his hands.

"I didn't know that Kimberly was an alcoholic. She didn't drink around me, at first."

"And then?"

"And then she started drinking. Because of me. It's my fault."

"You forced her to drink? You poured it down her throat?"

"No."

"Well, what then? Kimberly was a grown woman, a free agent. She was responsible for her own choices."

"You don't understand."

"Well, make me understand."

"It's my fault. I killed her."

"Merlin, why don't you let me check you into St. John's for a couple of days? I think you need some rest."

"No."

"Grief is a natural process, Merlin. It's supposed to hurt."

"Can I come back tomorrow?"

"Yes. I will make time for you. Come at five o'clock. I'm going to give you a prescription for sleeping pills. But you must not abuse them, Merlin. Will you promise me to take them only as prescribed?"

"Yes."

"All right. We'll see you tomorrow."

Merlin found his way out to the parking lot. He drove down the ramp and onto Wilshire Boulevard. He headed east away from the ocean. He wasn't going home. He was going to Kimberly's apartment. She had given him her key, although he had never yet actually been inside the building. He had picked her up and dropped her off a couple of times, and he knew the neighborhood.

Merlin turned down Sepulveda Boulevard and pulled up right behind Kimberly's green VW Rabbit.

He opened the front door to her first-story apartment and looked inside. The place was a wreck. By the wall to Merlin's right, as he walked in, was a cheap, black sofa. Clothes: bras, panties, stockings, shorts, and sweatshirts — were strewn across it, probably the residue of Kimberly's last-minute packing for Betty Ford.

He walked into her kitchen. The red light on her phone blinked. Merlin hit the button. Three different messages, all from Harvey Wilson, bleeped out, all asking where she was and pleading with her to call when she got home.

There was a partly consumed bottle of Smirnoff vodka on the shelf, next to the telephone. Merlin unscrewed the top and drank from it.

He opened the refrigerator door. Inside were cartons of

cottage cheese, milk, and yogurt. There was a half eaten apple and a jar of Peter Pan Peanut Butter. Merlin threw the apple and the milk into the trash and closed the door.

He took the vodka bottle with him into the bedroom. The room looked like it had been hit by an earthquake. Her bed, a mattress on the floor, was covered with clothes. The closet door stood open. Some of the dresses and coats had fallen off their hangers to the closet floor.

Merlin walked into the other room. There was an IBM PC mounted on a desk. Computer discs, books, magazines, tapes, LP sleeves, CDs, coffee cups, and Diet Coke cans, lay, scattered all around it. Bookcases lined the walls, and a tape and CD player stood on the opposite side of the room from the computer.

Merlin looked back at the computer. A manuscript lay next to it. He picked it up and read:

The Wizard of Jazz
The Autobiography of Merlin Black
by
Merlin Black
With Kimberly Gates.

CHAPTER ONE

America is a racist country. I was born in Memphis, Tennessee at a time when racism was neither subtle nor disguised. It was no accident that Martin Luther King was killed there by a white man. Black people in this country have been systematically brutalized. Our culture was destroyed. Our self-esteem was castrated. If you did not grow up in a country where you were detested for the color of your skin, then you cannot know how I feel."

What a strange sensation, Merlin thought. To read your own life, told in your own voice, but not written by you. Oh, I said those things. I'm sure of that. But to see them here in print that's different. They have such a formality and finality. I never thought of myself as a finished man, but more as a work-in-progress.

Merlin sank into Kimberly's chair. He drank the vodka and turned the pages. Kimberly had gotten it right. More or less. But she had left out things — important things. But then, those were the very things that Merlin had not told her.

My father was a lawyer. That made him a member of the black elite in Memphis. He wasn't no Medgar Evers exactly, but he was one of the 'Top Niggers in Town'. And he wasn't no Uncle Tom. He was outspoken. He told it like it was. The white motherfuckers could have shot him at any time, or dragged him off in the middle of the night.

Merlin remembered saying all these things. But he hadn't been thinking of what they would look like in print. Kimberly had tried to capture his voice, the way he actually talked. And to a large extent, she had succeeded. Merlin could turn the hip, ghetto dialect on or off at will, but, usually, during interviews, he kept it on. It made him feel tough, less vulnerable.

The vodka burned and numbed Merlin's tongue. He read on.

My mother was a scary person. She was very intelligent and very talented. She played the piano. It's mainly from her I get my musical interest. But she was ambitious and high-strung. Nowadays, she'd have had a career, but in those days, the wife of a lawyer didn't work. She was frustrated. She wanted more out of life.

Merlin read on. He read about how he was beaten up by white kids in Memphis. About Harriet and their two sons. About New York and Charlie Parker and heroin and Cheryl. Kimberly had done a lot of research outside their interviews. She talked about the various musical styles: swing, bebop, cool, hard bop, free jazz. She discussed the growth of rock and how it eclipsed much of jazz's audience. As jazz became more obscure, rock became more sophisticated.

Some of the younger musicians like John Coltrane, Merlin's former saxophonist, experimented relentlessly. But this subtle form of avant-garde jazz won few converts and, in fact, alienated most listeners who turned away from these dissonant and complex sounds. These alienated former jazz fans, too, joined the swelling audience of rock, which was also experimental, but much more accessible and seemingly more relevant to the 60's generation.

*****

Merlin put down the manuscript and looked around the room. The sun had set, and, although it was still early in the evening, he felt exhausted. He finished off the vodka, set the bottle on the floor, and stood up. He walked back into the bedroom.

Did it make him feel closer to Kimberly to be here, he wondered. Yes and no. He had never spent any time with her here. And there were no pictures of her on the walls. There was only one item on the bedroom dresser. It was a photograph of two little girls. Merlin assumed it was Kimberly and Natalie as children, although he could not be certain even of this.

He recognized some of her clothes: fuscia pyjamas of polyester charmeuse with cuffed sleeves, and a silk blouse of cobalt blue in a floral jacquard print. Innumerable other skirts, dresses, blouses, and sweaters hung in the closet or lay abandoned on the floor. But Merlin's eye fell on a wrap robe that Kimberly had once worn at his house — emerald green with a tie belt and a full chiffon collar. Short and with a deep v-neck; it came only half way down her thighs. Kimberly had looked sensational in it. It was perfect for her long, red, frizzy hair and pale skin.

Merlin gently took it off the hanger and held it to his face. He wanted to find her scent, and he did. That smell — whatever its components, that odor that was hers alone, overwhelmed him with memory and loss.

The way she looked, the things she did and said, those were locked away solidly in the vault of his memory forever. But the scent, the smell, the odor vanished. Even if you developed a vocabulary for its musty fragrance, perfume: earthy and sweet, salty, flowery, or pungent. Those were only words, and only the smell itself could bring the person back to you. How long, Merlin wondered, would her scent linger on these clothes?

Merlin grasped the robe to his chest and sank to Kimberly's mattress on the floor. He didn't undress or even take off his shoes. His head hit the pillow. He lay on his side and pulled his knees toward his face. He clutched Kimberly's robe and inhaled as much of her as he could, until weariness overcame him, and he slept.

The Dream

Merlin flew above the streets of his childhood, over his high school. The landmarks were familiar, but the colors different — wild and garish: purple, crimson, bright orange, turquoise, gray, and black. He had never been fond of school, but the ninth grade, so far, had been the worst yet. He was smaller than most of the kids and was often the target of the bullies.

He flew to the new home, in the white neighborhood. He tried to fly again, but he couldn't. He would have to walk. His feet felt as if they had weights attached to them. His steps were slow and difficult. He had to run the gauntlet of the white bullies who resented his intrusion into their territory.

His father always blamed him. Merlin had a temper that always seemed to get him into trouble, but he wasn't stupid. He didn't enjoy getting hurt, and he would avoid it if possible.

He saw the slanting, red-shingled gable of the new house, the front porch with an overhanging roof. Merlin missed the old neighborhood, and Harriet and his other friends. He did not like being the only black family in the neighborhood. He did not like the hatred he saw in the eyes of the white people.

"Why are you so late, son?" Sarah Black asked.

The room was dark. She had pulled all the shades down. Merlin tried not to look at her. He stared at the piano, intensely aware of her presence. Finally, he turned his gaze and saw her on the sofa, wearing nothing but an emerald green robe.

Kimberly's robe.

Sarah was smiling, showing off her dimples. She was beautiful. She was the most beautiful woman Merlin had ever seen. She was, in fact, all of the women he had ever loved. She was Harriet and Cheryl and Tara and Kimberly.

Merlin could see the line between her full breasts, the soft, light-brown breasts of his own mother.

The odor of whiskey permeated the room. She got this way when she'd been drinking. And then, when she was sober it was like it had never happened. She was prim and proper, every inch the fine lady she imagined herself to be.

Merlin wanted her. His cock was stiff with longing for his own mother. She wanted him too. Again. But, at the same time, he knew it was wrong. They had never talked about it.

169

Afterwards. Merlin felt confused. Desire and repulsion. An overwhelming need to be there. His erection felt enormous.

"Why are you so late, son?" Sarah Black repeated.

"I had to stay after school to practise my trumpet," he said.

"Good. I want you to be a musician and to play real pretty. Girls will love you if you play beautiful music. Come here."

"Yes, ma'am," Merlin said, but he didn't budge.

"Come over here and sit by me."

Merlin came over and sat on the side of the sofa. His mother ran her hand through his kinky hair.

"You know that you're my little man, don't you?"

"Yes ma'am."

Sarah picked up the glass next to the half empty bottle on the coffee table and drank down the brown liquor.

"Your father is a bad man. You know that, don't you?"

"Yes, ma'am." Merlin didn't want to look into his mother's eyes. He kept looking down. But what he saw were her breasts. He was afraid that she would notice his erection.

"He's not very nice to me. He beats me and treats me mean. You know that, don't you?"

"Yes, ma'am."

"So you have to be my little man. My hero. Will you do that?"

"Yes, ma'am."

"You know he killed your brother, don't you?"

"Yes, ma'am."

"He wanted to kill you, too. I protected you," Sarah said. "And now you have to protect me. Will you do that?"

"Yes."

Sarah drank more whisky. Her mood changed. She seemed suddenly happy and frivolous.

"You know why I named you Merlin, don't you?"

"Yes."

"Well, tell me. I want to hear you say it."

"Merlin was a very wise man. A magician and a wizard."

"And what did he do?"

"He brought huge stones from Ireland and set them up in England."

"And what else did he do?"

"He built the Round Table for King Arthur and helped him select the fifty knights who got to sit at it."

"Who was his mother?"

"His mother was a princess."

"That's right. And who was his father?"

"A demon."

"That's right. And what kind of a demon was his father?"

"I don't know."

"You don't know?" Sarah smiled broadly.

"He was an incubus." She pinched his cheek.

"Say, what?"

"An incubus. Do you know what an incubus is?"

"No, ma'am."

Sarah put her hand on Merlin's erect penis and began to stroke it.

"An incubus is a demon who comes to ladies in the night. And he takes this little bone, like you've got here." Sarah grabbed Merlin's cock harder and wiggled it back and forth, inside his blue jeans. "Then he pokes it inside ladies while they're sleeping. Take your pants off, and I'll show you."

Merlin stood up and unzipped his jeans. His mother helped him to pull them down around his ankles. He stepped out of them, and then she pulled down his underpants as well.

She untied her robe. She was not wearing anything under it.

"Now, come on back here," she said. "And pretend like you're an incubus. I'll show you where to put it."

Merlin already knew where to put it. But he also knew his mother wanted to pretend like this had never happened before. She guided him inside her. Merlin knew this was wrong. But it felt good. He liked being inside Sarah. It felt warm. She guided him gently in and out, back and forth.

"This is what an incubus does to a lady while she's sleeping. And when she wakes up, she doesn't remember anything. It was just a pleasant dream."

Merlin dreamed. He felt love for every woman he had ever known. Even if it wasn't right. Or maybe *because* it wasn't right. He didn't care. It was too big; it was beyond right and wrong, good and bad. It felt better and better.

He blinked and saw Cheryl. He blinked again and saw Kimberly. He felt a huge tidal wave inside him rock and roar into a spasm. He blinked again and looked into the face of his mother, as his sperm erupted back into her womb, the womb which had nurtured him, from which he had emerged, and from which he had first seen the light of day.

"Well, this is a breakthrough, Merlin." Dr. Dover seemed almost happy.

"It just came back to me in the dream. I guess I tried not to think about it."

"It's called repression."

"I know your goddamn, honky psychiatric jargon, Doc!"

"You're feeling anger, right now. That's good. Let it out."

"You're goddamn right, I'm feeling anger, now!"

"Are you angry with me?"

"No." Merlin slumped back down in his chair. Grief and alcohol were taking a toll. Merlin had not slept well. He would have to fill his prescription for sleeping pills. He needed some rest.

"I don't know who to be angry at. My mother fucked me. Or I fucked her. I'm not sure which."

"How old were you, Merlin?"

"Fourteen."

"Then you were sexually abused by your mother. It was her fault. You were a child, and she was an adult. She was your mother. You were supposed to do what she told you to do."

"I always remembered that she was crazy. But I forgot how crazy. Why would anyone do shit like that."

"You'd be surprised how common it is. There are more cases of fathers raping their daughters. But there are countless cases of mothers abusing their sons. People would be shocked if they knew just how common it really is."

"Is that supposed to make me feel better?"

"Well, Merlin, I think it explains a lot."

"Yeah? Like what?"

"Your ambivalent feelings toward women, for instance."

"I ain't ambivalent about women. I love women."

"Do you, Merlin? I hear a lot of anger, a lot of contempt, in your voice, when you talk about 'the bitches'."

"That's because you ain't been called 'nigger' all your life."

"No, Merlin. I haven't. That's true. So you don't think this revelation explains anything?"

"I don't want explanations, Doc. I want to feel better. No. No, this just makes me feel worse. Like I don't got enough to feel bad about with Kimberly. I gotta be responsible for my own mother as well."

"You're not responsible for either, Merlin."

"The fuck, you say!"

"Merlin, what do you expect from me?"

"I expect you to stop the pain."

"I can't do that, Merlin."

"What am I paying you for, then?"

"The only way you can stop the pain is to go through it, experience it, feel it. The more you try to obliterate it, the worse it will get."

"Shit! I don't know why I put up with this jive-ass bullshit. I'm outta here."

Merlin was on his feet and half way to the door.

"I can still put you up at St. John's for a couple of days, Merlin. It might be good for you."

"And you might try a vibrator up your ass, Doc. It just might be good for you!"

Merlin exploded out of the room and slammed the door behind him.

"Can I set up another appointment for you, Mr Black?"

Merlin looked at the perky, neat receptionist behind the desk. Something about her complacency, her serenity, her calm, bovine, patronizing efficiency infuriated Merlin. He gave her a withering stare and belligerently pushed the appointment book off the ledge and onto the floor.

He stormed out of the office, and took the elevator to the first floor. He found the pharmacy and had his prescription for sleeping pills filled.

"Will that be all, Mr Black?"

"Yes." Merlin handed his *Visa* credit card to the woman behind the counter.

"Your doctor explained these, didn't he?"

"Say, what?"

"Be sure and follow the directions. Only one every night and don't mix them with alcohol."

"I can read, bitch. And if I want a sermon, I'll call Jerry Falwell."

The sun had begun to set, as Merlin pulled his blood-red Jaguar to a halt in his driveway. He picked up Kimberly's manuscript, which he had brought with him from her apartment and left on the passenger seat of his car during the session with Dr. Dover.

He walked inside his black and white Malibu house and put the manuscript down on the table next to the telephone. He noticed that the red light of his voice machine was blinking, and so he punched it in.

"Merlin, this is Peter Pollard. Call me. Right now. Not later. Right now. I mean it." This was Peter's equivalent of a violently emotional scene. There was a slight pause, and then Peter's voice said: "I love you, man." And then the click and the pause, and the whirl, as the tape rolled back into place.

"Oh, hi, Maria," Merlin said, after calling Peter's number. "Where's your redneck husband?"

"Merlin! He just stepped out for a minute, but he's worried about you. He said you were supposed to call him yesterday."

"Guilty as charged. But I'll be at the house for a while."

"Okay, Merlin. I'll tell him you called."

Merlin went behind the bar, and, before he had time to think about it, he glanced into the mirror. He looked terrible. He was still wearing the white suit and black t-shirt that he had been wearing for three days now, ever since Kimberly's funeral. He had not shaved, and white whiskers, like blemishes, sprouted all over his face.

He had not bothered to wear the wig lately, and he had taken off the dark glasses when he walked in the door. His eyes were bloodshot and weary. His wrinkles looked like exhausted mounds of sagging flesh. His whole face seemed to be drooping; gravity pulling each feature downward toward the earth. He averted his gaze away from the mirror and toward the liquor cabinet and grabbed a fifth of vodka.

He put his dark glasses back on, as he walked outside the back door and down the steps to the beach. He sat down and watched the boiling red sun sink into the aquamarine Pacific Ocean like a lobster being lowered to its doom. One could almost hear the sizzle, as the sacrificial sun met its watery death.

We need music for this, Merlin thought. The last movement of Beethoven's ninth or a Bach fugue. Merlin loved Bach. He had tapes of the *Brandenberg Concertos*, the cello suites, the partitas for keyboard, *The Art of Fugue*, the *Goldberg Variations*, *The Musical Offering*, as well as various organ works.

174

He played that music over and over. It was so pure. So remote from the world that he knew, the world of race hatred, the constant bickering of women and agents and record company executives. The world of traffic and smog and noise and drug addiction and hangovers. It belonged to a world set apart, a world beyond suffering, a world where only the music mattered, and it was *above* all the debris of human life.

He admired Bach for that. The timelessness of it. Merlin knew that his own music existed in concrete slabs of time and history. It boomed out from the particulars of the life that he, himself, had led. It exploded from the hectic, manic bustle of World War II; it roared out from the disenchantment that blacks and others felt during the McCarthy Era, the fanatical anti-Communist world of the 1950's, where everything and everyone different from 'Ozzie' and 'Harriet' were suspect or despised.

His music communicated the joy of anticipation when the civil rights movement began. It reflected also the sadness that many felt when that dream turned to dust. When Martin Luther King lay dead and bleeding on the balcony of the Lorraine Hotel in Memphis. His own Memphis.

Merlin's music commented on the cynicism of the 70's and the greed of the 80's. It was not ethereal like the music of Bach. It was sensual and earthy. It was about how people sweat when their bodies are jerking and writhing in sexual union. About the confusion of a people and a culture gone wrong. About the despair of a people who had lost God and, what's worse, had lost hope.

Who needs hope when you got ninety-five channels on your stereo color TV? Who needs God when you got computerized house-cleaning and guaranteed perfect sex with a machine? Virtual Fucking Reality. "Not the real thing, but an INCREDIBLE simulation!"

Merlin did not know what the 90's had in store for America, but he was not optimistic. Everything was perfect. Perfectly dead. Everywhere he looked he saw death. No one seemed to care any more. Once there was a time when America looked forward to a better future. Now it was enough to look around and point your finger. As if to ask: "What went wrong?"

No one wanted to fix things any more; they just wanted to

blame someone else for the carnage. America's defunct, kaput. A corpse — decaying, decomposing, putrefying. The body cannot be revived, or resurrected, or brought back to life in any way. Our only interest now is to wait around for the results of the autopsy.

My own people are no better, Merlin thought. Where's the passion that we saw in Martin Luther King and Malcolm X? Where is the commitment to change? All gone. All gone into the pseudo-respectability of the black middle class and the despair of the crack-smoking inhabitants of the ghettos, those bombed-out remains of our cities which hang on somehow as eyesores, blemishes, cancers of a world without conscience, communities without hope.

It was dark now. The sun had completely gone down, and the moon had not yet come up. The air was cooler, but Merlin had his vodka to keep him warm.

A shadow stumbled into his line of vision: an old woman. Merlin could not, at first, make out any of her features. She seemed stoned. She couldn't walk straight. His, was a private beach. Homeless people weren't supposed to be here.

"Hey, man," she said.

"What?" Merlin replied.

She moved closer toward him. She was a white woman in her 50's, younger than Merlin, probably. But she looked ancient. She was wearing a long, shapeless garment of the kind they used to call a granny dress.

"What city is this?" She swayed back and forth, squinting, as if trying to focus her gaze on Merlin.

"This is Malibu."

"Malibu? What kinda place is that?" She drank from a bottle of cheap, red wine.

"A place for rich people. Famous people." Merlin drank from his bottle of imported vodka. Then he held it up in her direction, making a friendly gesture, saluting her.

"Cheers!" he said.

"Well, cheers to you, good Samaritan. Are you a rich person?"

"Sometimes."

"Sometimes? What does that mean?"

"I've had my ups and downs."

"Mind if I sit down?" Without waiting for a reply, the

woman plopped down in the sand next to Merlin. She had a strong and unpleasant odor.

"Don't mind if I do," she said, as if answering her own question. "So, you're rich, are you? Are you famous, too?"

"My name is Merlin Black."

"Never heard of ya. Hi," she said and hiccuped.

"Hi," Merlin said and shook her hand.

"I'm a musician. A trumpet player."

"Zat a fack? I used to play the accordion."

"Any good?"

"Good? Shit! I was the best fucking accordion player in Albuquerque, New Mexico. Probably the best fucking accordion player Albuquerque ever had. Listen, could you spare some change? I haven't eaten in days."

Merlin looked at her. Her clothes were little more than rags. Her face, sunburned and full of sores. He reached into his back pocket and, as he did, he looked away from the woman.

He pulled out his wallet, and, as he turned his gaze back in her direction, he saw a pair of silver scissors, hurling down toward his arm. The scissors struck him in the middle of his left forearm. The pain was sharp and immediate. He dropped the wallet in the sand. Before he realized what was happening, the woman grabbed his wallet and stood up. Merlin clutched his wounded arm with his right hand and made a motion in the woman's direction. She kicked him in the chin.

"Fucking-nigger-shit!" she said and took off, running down the beach, at full speed.

Merlin forced himself onto his feet with the intention of pursuing her, but something held him back. The woman had already been swallowed up by the darkness. Her bottle of wine had been turned over and now spilled its contents into the sand. Like a glass animal, bleeding to death.

The cut from the scissors seemed deep. Merlin took off his coat, rolled up his sleeve, and looked at the wound. It was too dark to see anything. He picked up the vodka bottle, poured some of the liquid on his arm, and then took a generous swig.

Shit! he thought. Here I was feeling sorry for the old bitch. Merlin picked up his coat and walked back inside. He went into the bathroom and turned on the light. The wound was not that serious, but it hurt. He put a Band-Aid on it to stop the bleeding.

Then he picked up the coat, which he had laid by the sink and heard something rattle in his side pocket. He reached for the object and pulled out the bottle of sleeping pills he had just had filled at the pharmacy. Maybe that would help stop the pain, he thought. He unscrewed the top, pulled out the cotton, and teased a pink pill into the palm of his hand. He popped it in his mouth and washed it down with vodka.

ONE. He walked back into his living room. It was still full of musical instruments. There had been no rehearsals since Kimberly's death, and he had no idea when, if ever, he would perform again. He sat down by the lamp and picked up the manuscript. He found the place where he had quit, the night before, and began to read again.

In the late 1960's, I began to think that jazz was becoming irrelevant. All the young black kids were listening to Sly Stone, James Brown, and Jimi Hendrix. I wanted to make music that young people, especially young, black people would want to listen to.

So, I got together some hip musicians who played funky instruments, electronic instruments. And we were making some very together music. We decided to go public with it. So, we played this gig at Carnegie Hall. But a lot of people didn't understand what we were trying to do. They thought we were selling out.

This first gig at Carnegie Hall was a disaster. It ended in a riot. But later, we kept playing our new type of Fusion Jazz. And finally, people began to dig it. It caught on, real big.

It was a crazy time, the late 1960's. There was a lot of heavy shit going down.

There were gaps and blank spaces in the manuscript. Merlin realized Kimberly meant to come back and fill them in.

I never was much into religion. I grew up in the South. I loved the music. That gospel music was some heavy shit, man. It turned a lot of folks on. But I didn't much dig what the preachers were putting down. You know what I mean? All those 'Thou shalt nots'?

Personally, I admired Dr. King very much. The stuff he was doing then. But I did not accept the religious part of it.

Merlin felt uncomfortable with all this. Sure, he had said it. And at the time, he had meant it. Day after day and week after week he had spewed it out for Kimberly. He realized now that part of it was a pose. He was flirting with Kimberly, trying to make her think he was important. And now it seemed so, well… arrogant.

As he read his own life in his own conversational style, the words haunted him, accused him, mocked him, condemned him. It was the human part that Merlin had ignored. That's what was missing. And it was the human part that he was acutely aware of now. How he had used people — his mother, his father, Harriet. He felt sorrow especially for his sons, Benjamin who was dead and Eugene who hated him.

Merlin decided to take another sleeping pill. He got up and went back to the bathroom. He picked up the bottle and looked at it. Then he took off the cap and shook another capsule into his palm. He placed it on his tongue and swallowed.

TWO. Merlin put the pills in his pants pocket. The phone rang. Merlin didn't answer it. He heard Peter's voice coming through the message box:

"Merlin? Pick up. Shit, I can't believe I've missed you again. I really want to talk to you tonight. Please call. Even if it's late. I've been thinking about you. I know you're in pain. Call me. Bye."

Merlin took another long drink from the vodka bottle. He sat down and read again.

When Martin Luther King died, it was the end of an era for a lot of us. We had hoped. He made us hope that things could change, get better. I had gone to Memphis to march with him and in behalf of the striking sanitation workers. That march had turned into a police riot: the white, motherfucking cops of Memphis, beating up on everybody. They killed my youngest son, Benjamin. I can never forgive them for that. We were all looking forward to the next march, the one that never took place. Not, that is, until after Martin had been killed too.

Merlin remembered two funerals — Benjamin's graveside service, attended by so few. And the one on TV: the mule cart, the poor people, the crowds along the road, the widow, the children — the genuine grief and despair he saw in those faces. He had been deeply moved. He had felt guilty at some of the cheap shots he had made against preachers. Against Martin and Malcolm X and their "white" religions.

Why was he, Merlin, so cynical? When actually *had* he lost his religion. He realized now it had something to do with his mother. She had been religious. She had believed. But, look how she acted. Merlin wondered if Kimberly were still alive, if he would have the guts to admit to her that he had slept with his own mother.

The idea still made Merlin very uncomfortable. No, not just uncomfortable. The idea made him sick. It spoiled what little desire he had left to live.

He realized, as he shook two more capsules into his hand, that it was no longer about getting a good night's rest.

THREE. FOUR. And Cheryl? What was that all about? He read the facts in Kimberly's book. That's how he had begun to think of it. It was Kimberly's book. And it was a lie, a fiction. He could write the real book, now. He could. But he wouldn't.

Cheryl had saved his life. He would have died thirty-six years earlier if it hadn't been for Cheryl. Maybe that would have been for the best. No. No. He could not let go of the notion that it was good that he had lived to know Cheryl. And Tara. And Kimberly. Good. But painful. Why did it all have to hurt so much?

He had neglected Cheryl. He had beat her and cheated on her. And when she finally left, long after a sane woman would have, he felt a great void. It was because he loved her. But he had put everything else first. Every time he thought of Cheryl, he ached. The ache was real. But what did it mean? Merlin could no longer distinguish between desire and despair, between lust and guilt.

FIVE. And Tara? Well, Tara could take care of herself. She was a survivor. He had treated her badly too. Why? It was partly that male-macho-ego shit. And where had he learned that? From his father?

SIX. The room was growing dark. Merlin turned out the light. He couldn't read any longer. The prince of darkness was in his

180

element. He was blind in the light, blinded by the light. In the darkness, he could see. But he did not like what he saw. The darkness of his soul. And he began to wonder if he'd been wrong. If there was a god. And he began to ask questions of this hypothetical god.

Why have I come to this? Am I evil? Was it supposed to be this way?

Again there was only silence.

SEVEN. Kimberly. She came from nowhere. A gift. He had been pompous and rude to her. But she wanted his story. And then she wanted him. He had no doubt that she loved him. Or that he loved her. That hypothetical god. Why would He give Merlin such a treasure, only to snatch her away.

It seems, he thought, that everything I did for her was wrong. For me, she started to drink again. For me, she went to the Betty Ford Clinic. For me, she probably left and died.

The worst thing is that I can't get the image of her out of my head. The last time I saw her alive. At the clinic. Walking away from me: mad, defiant, bitter, unforgiving. I said I would come to see her, and she said: "Don't bother." I asked her to call me. She said: "Don't hold your breath!" The last words I ever heard her say.

EIGHT. The phone rang again: "Okay, Merlin. I know you're there. Pick up. No? I'm coming over. If you do something stupid, man, I'll never forgive you." Click. Whirl.

Not much time, now.

NINE. How odd. After all his venom against women and whites. That his only two friends were a white woman and a white man. The only ones who really cared. Peter wants to save me. Even now. Sorry to disappoint you, Peter.

TEN. Merlin the magician has just run out of tricks. No more magic. All gone. Oh, I could live on with declining talent and deteriorating health. But I don't want to. With me, it was never about survival. The party's over, and I don't want to wait around for the hangover. One of the perks of suicide: you don't have to worry about the morning after.

"The Wizard has Fizzled." Isn't that what that fucking

critic said: "The Wizard has Fizzled?"

ELEVEN. I seem to remember that the Merlin in the King Arthur stories lived his life backwards. I think mama used to say that. He was born with all his faculties, his talents, his memory. And as he got older, he got younger, more immature, less talented. He remembered only the future, not the past.

TWELVE. I think mama told me that. Poor lady. You lived your life in fantasy. You hated your husband, who beat you and mistreated you. So, you made your son your dream lover. Your prince. I was supposed to come to your rescue, to save you. And all I did was run away. From you, from Harriet, my sons, from Tara and, finally, from Kimberly.

THIRTEEN. Just for the sake of tooting sounds through a misshapen piece of brass. Ta-TAAAA! Ta-Ta-Ta — TAAAAA! Don't even have one, anymore. Left the last one in a graveyard next to a white god on a stone cross.

FOURTEEN. Things are getting fuzzy now. It's supposed to get dark, isn't it? But it actually seems lighter. The whites are gonna get me in the end, after all. I've avoided them all these years. Ran away from Buster and those other punk kids in Memphis. Miserable motherfuckers! I wonder what... No. No. I don't want to go this way. Bad form. Give the people what they want. Make your audience happy. Pray to the white god.

FIFTEEN. The one who hates and torments me.

SIXTEEN. Makes my fucking life miserable.

SEVENTEEN. In the name of the Father.

EIGHTEEN. And the Son.

NINETEEN. And the Holy Fucking Ghost.

TWENTY. Amen.

August 29-31, 1990

He stood at the pinnacle of a large building, a skyscraper. He had a choice. He could jump or he could stay. If he jumped, he knew that he would not be hurt. For it was only a dream.

He jumped. He saw the traffic on the streets far down below. It looked like mid-town Manhattan from the Empire State Building. The sun blinded him, becoming fuzzy and indistinct. It materialized into shapes. Demons. Monsters. Then, it took on human forms: the orb like a face, the corona like a halo. The face came into focus. It was Peter Pollard.

"Peter?"

"Merlin! Welcome back."

"Where am I?"

"The UCLA Hospital."

"You saved me again?"

"Yes. Are you going to thank me?"

"I dunno. I was dreaming."

Merlin tried to focus his eyes. Everything was a sterile white. The walls, the ceiling, the sheets. Even his visitor was wearing a white shirt and a white bandanna.

"Well, you better," Peter said, " 'cause this is the last time." He smiled, suggesting he didn't really mean it.

Merlin tried to sit up. Peter forced him back on the bed.

"No, Merlin. Stay down. Doctor's orders."

"The dream was trying to tell me something, Peter. I'm just too groggy to think."

"Then stop thinking. Maybe, that's what you need."

"Okay, Peter. Whatever you say."

Merlin closed his eyes. He slept. When he awakened, there was a nurse. She wanted him to eat. Merlin wasn't hungry.

"How long have I been here?" he asked.

"Two days. Don't you remember?"

"No," he said.

He managed to eat a little of the clear broth. The brightness of the room hurt. He closed his eyes.

He seemed to be dead. He was lying on a funeral bier, and the swirling bodies circled all around him. Charlie Parker stuck his face right into Merlin's and laughed at him.

"You're too soft, Merlin," he said. "You've got to be tough

183

in this business."

Cheryl looked at him with anger and hurt.

"I thought you'd call," she said. "Why didn't you call?"

Then his son Benjamin looked down on him smirking in utter contempt.

"Why didn't you save me? You could've saved me."

"Yeah, me too." It was Kimberly. He was glad to see her. But she didn't seem glad to see him.

"I'm still pissed at you. If you'd of come with me to Betty Ford like I asked you, this never would have happened."

Merlin tried to move, but was immobile. He tried to speak, but couldn't. He wanted to scream. If he just tried hard enough, he knew he could. He was certain of it. And then he *was* screaming. A nurse opened the door. Not the same nurse who was there earlier. This one was younger and prettier.

"Where's Peter?" Merlin asked.

"Who?"

"Peter Pollard."

"Look, Mr Black," the nurse said, "it's two o'clock. You can't have a visitor in the middle of the night."

"Oh."

Merlin was too weak to fight.

"Is there anything else I can get for you, Mr Black?"

"No."

Merlin didn't want to go to sleep for fear he would dream again. But the nurse turned off the light. It was dark again. Just rest, he told himself. Don't struggle. Just relax.

"Is there anything I can get for you, Merlin?"

Merlin opened his eyes. It was Peter again.

"Why do you put up with me, Peter?"

"What kind of question is that, Merlin?"

"I've never brought you anything but trouble."

"That's not true. I choose to be by you. Nobody's holding a gun to my head. Your music is the inspiration of my life. If I hadn't known you, my world would have been poorer by half."

"Peter?"

"Yes, Merlin."

"There is something I want."

"Name it."

"Kimberly's manuscript. In my living room."

"We have you set up, right here, Mr Black," the slim, middle-aged woman said.

He had never visited a book signing, much less been the honoree. He really wanted a drink, but he had promised Peter he wouldn't have one until after. Merlin had dressed in a black suit and white silk shirt. Peter had brought his wife Maria and young Merlin with them for the event. *The Wizard of Jazz: The Autobiography of Merlin Black* by Merlin Black and Kimberly Gates (Merlin changed the 'with' to 'and') had just arrived in bookstores, and Merlin had come to Brentano's to promote it.

A year had passed since Kimberly's death, and Merlin never stopped thinking about her. He still felt responsible. Merlin the magician had been able to banish pain, make it disappear through drugs, music, and cynicism, until one day the magic had stopped. The anguish had engulfed him like a tidal wave. The autobiography had forced him to focus.

"Why don't you sit down now, Merlin," Peter said.

Merlin sat in a blue institutional chair behind a long, flat table piled with copies of the autobiography. Maria took young Merlin and pulled him over to the side of the store.

"When are we going to play again, Peter?" Merlin asked.

"Whenever you say, Merlin. I'm ready."

"I'm sorry," Merlin said to the lady in charge. "Would you tell me your name again?"

"Maxfield. Morgan Maxfield. Call me Morgan."

"So how does this work exactly, Morgan?"

"Well," she said in her brisk and efficient sort of way. She seemed slightly nervous, slightly afraid of Merlin, who was not her typical sort of author. "First, we open the door."

She pointed outside the store to the open-air shopping center, where a line was already forming.

"They come in. You read a short passage. They buy a book and tell me what they want you to write in it. I'll jot it down on a piece of paper and hand it over to you."

"How about a dress rehearsal?" Peter said. "Sell me a book."

"Okay."

Ms. Morgan Maxfield walked Peter over to the counter and took his credit card. Peter walked back to the table, picked up a book, and opened it for Merlin.

Merlin picked up a pen, and wrote on the inside cover:

For Peter, my guardian angel.
Thank you for saving my life.
Twice.
Love Merlin.

"Can I open the door, now?" Morgan asked.

"Sure," Merlin said.

Peter grabbed his book and moved to the side of the store beside Maria and young Merlin. The crowd filed in with only a minimum of fuss.

"Hi," Morgan said to the crowd. "We are honored to have Merlin Black with us tonight, signing copies of his new book, *The Wizard of Jazz*. Mr Black, would you honor us with a reading?"

"No, Merlin said. "But I'll say a few words. This book was really written by Kimberly Gates, who died a year ago. She deserves the credit. She told it like it was. Mainly. I can't say I'm proud of everything in here." Merlin picked up a copy of the book. "I wasn't always nice to people. And I ain't proud of that. I just tried to make the best music I could."

The people in the audience began to clap.

"It ain't nothing to applaud about. What I'm trying to say is… I came to a place. A time in my life, where I couldn't hear the music. And all I could do was see how I had hurt people. And I wanted to die. But with the help of some friends…"

Merlin looked over at Peter and his family. He stretched out his arm, the book still in it, in their direction.

"These good people right here, in fact. If you want to applaud, applaud them."

The people did as Merlin bid them. Peter, smiling ironically, took a bow. Maria and little Merlin just looked embarrassed.

"They helped me understand that if I really wanted to atone, the best way I could do that was through my music. So, Merlin Black is back in business. And look out, 'cause I'm gonna be coming at ya, any time now."

As Merlin looked out at his audience, he noticed two familiar figures, a skinny man and a very large woman. He got up from his chair and walked over to them.

"Mr and Mrs Gates. Thank you for coming."

"Vivian," Mrs Gates said. "Call me, Vivian."

"Come on up to the front desk with me," Merlin said and gave his arm to the wobbly Vivian Gates.

As he guided her up to the table, she whispered in his ear.

"You said you'd finish her book, and you did. Thank you. Kimberly would be very proud. Very proud, indeed."

Morgan provided chairs for Vivian and Don Gates, and all sat down at the table. Merlin kept his head down signing books, with Morgan passing him slips of paper with the desired inscriptions. He received a slip that read:

> To his glorious
> Second wife,
> From a worthless
> Son of a bitch.

Merlin looked up into the smiling face of Tara Marlowe. Her face was older but still beautiful. As usual, she was dressed to perfection, a white, silk blouse and an original Liz Claiborne, taupe suit.

"Tara!"

He got up and embraced her.

"Thanks for coming," he said.

"You know I wouldn't miss an opportunity to embarrass you."

"You look great, Tara. Are you happy?"

"Yes, Merlin. How about you? Are you happy?"

"Well, Tara. I'm working on it. I've got some heavy karma hanging over me. But I'm trying."

"Good, Merlin. You know we were friends before we were lovers. We were lousy lovers. But we were pretty good friends. I'm still your friend, Merlin. Do you believe me?"

"Yes."

Merlin tried to keep the tears from his eyes. He had felt so isolated in the past few years. Perhaps most of his life.

"I brought somebody with me, Merlin."

"Who?"

A middle-aged black man with a receding hair line stood before him. He wore a conservative navy blue suit.

"Hi, dad."

"Gene."

"I hope you don't mind that I came."

"Mind? Shit!"

Merlin was no longer able to keep back the tears. The two men embraced.

"It wasn't really that I blamed you for Benjamin's death," Eugene began. But he was stopped by a catch in his throat.

"You don't have to say anything," Merlin said.

"No, I do. I know you're not responsible for what happened to Benjamin. I just hated you because you loved him more."

"I have a lot to answer for."

"No, you don't. Let's start over. Okay?"

"Okay."

Merlin did the best he could to finish the book signings. He was glad that he had agreed to come. It had turned out much better than he'd expected. Later, he'll go out to eat with Peter and his family. He'll ask Tara and Mr and Mrs Gates, but they will probably refuse. Maybe Gene will go with them. They won't patronize any of the places he used to frequent with Kimberly. Maybe a nice little Italian restaurant in Hollywood.

Later he'll have to return to his lonely house in Malibu. He should sell the place. There were too many unhappy memories there. He wanted to play music again. Not for money. Not for fame. That was the destructive part. He wanted to play again because he enjoyed it. How easy it was to forget that jazz is fun. It doesn't matter whether it's the Lighthouse or the Hollywood Bowl or the sidewalk of Sunset Boulevard.

He remembered an excited boy in Memphis who turned on his radio to 'The Sounds of Harlem'. He remembered the thrill of hearing Cootie Williams blowing a golden trumpet. He smiled and signed one more book:

To Jennie Moore.
Best Wishes for a long
And prosperous life,
Merlin Black.

END